Infini-D™
Revealed

BRENDAN DONAHOE

ADAM LAVINE

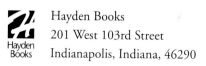

Hayden Books
201 West 103rd Street
Indianapolis, Indiana, 46290

Infini-D™ Revealed

©1996 Brendan Donahoe and Adam Lavine

Library of Congress Catalog Number: 95-80294
ISBN: 1-56830-222-3

Copyright © 1996 Hayden Books

Printed in the United States of America 1 2 3 4 5 6 7 8 9 0

Warning and Disclaimer

Publisher	Lyn Blake
Editor-in-Chief	Michael Nolan
Managing Editor	Lisa Wilson

Production/Copy Editor
Bront Davis

Publishing Coordinator
Rosemary Lewis

Acquisitions Editor
Karen Whitehouse

Development Editor
Dennis Hamilton

Production Team Supervisor
Laurie Casey

Book Design
Gary Adair

Cover Design
Karen Ruggles

Graphic Image Specialists
Clint Lahnen
Sonja Hart
Laura Robbins

Production Team
Heather Butler
Angela Calvert
Kim Cofer
Aleata Howard
Erika Millen
Karen Walsh

Indexer
Bront Davis

Production Analysts
Jason Hand
Bobbi Satterfield

About the Authors

Brendan Donohoe has been creating 3D images and animation with Specular Infini-D since version 1.1. Currently living in Amherst, Massachusetts, he has attended Hampshire College on and off since 1993 and has been working at Specular for the same period of time. At Specular, he works closely with all of Specular's products, helping to ensure their continued reliability. Brendan is also one third of the team that brought Specular onto the World Wide Web.

Adam Lavine began working in 3D in 1987 at the Center for Knowledge Communication at UMass, Amherst, where he produced educational animation for children. He is a coauthor of the original version of Infini-D, and a co-founder of Specular. Before founding Specular, Adam held a variety of jobs, including juggler, newspaper editor, and computer technician. Currently, he is President and Chief Executive Officer of Specular International, located in Amherst, Massachusetts.

Trademark Acknowledgments

All terms mentioned in this book that are known to be trademarks or services marks have been appropriately capitalized. Hayden Books cannot attest to the accuracy of this information. Use of a term in this book should not be regarded as affecting the validity of any trademark or service mark. Infini-D is a trademark of Specular, Inc.

Cover illustration by Daniel Sroka. This illustration contains models from: Blimp and Earth ©1996 by Tim Landry (Dream Quest Images); Fox News ©1996 by Randy Cates (Computer Animation and Design); Robot from Cyberball ©1996 by Scott Wells; Castle Cellar ©1996 by Ben Spees; Island, Seashell, and Eagle ©1996 by Brian Wyser. The 1995 Tony Awards logo by C. David Piña ©1995 Smith-Hemion Productions.

Acknowledgments

A special thanks to

David Stokes, who used his extensive Infini-D experience to help write Chapter 10, devised a number of clever Infini-D tricks (many of which are scattered throughout the following pages), and without whose help this book would never have been finished on time.

Katherine Brady, who helped with some preliminary editing, got Brendan's writing gears oiled again, and without whose moral support this book never would have been finished on time.

All the folks at Specular International, who encouraged us, offered plenty of suggestions, and without whose award-winning software this book never would have been written.

Hayden Books

The staff of Hayden Books is committed to bringing you the best computer books. What our readers think of Hayden is important to our ability to serve our customers. If you have any comments, no matter how great or how small, we'd appreciate you taking the time to send us a note.

You can reach Hayden Books at the following:

Hayden Books
201 West 103rd Street
Indianapolis, IN 46290
(800) 428-5331 voice
(800) 448-3804 fax

Email addresses:

America Online: Hayden Bks
Internet: hayden@hayden.com

Visit the Hayden Books Web site at
http://www.hayden.com

Contents at a Glance

Table of Contents

Part II Essential Infini-D

4 Working with the Workshop   59

Introduction to the World of Infini-D

1

If you are new to Infini-D and 3D graphics, then you are about to discover a whole new dimension of artistic and visual expression. If you are a seasoned Infini-D user, then this book will reveal tips, examples, and secrets that will make you work more quickly and efficiently and expand your repertoire of Infini-D techniques. Regardless of your skill level, you'll emerge from this book with a wealth of ideas, techniques, and effects from some of the world's top Infini-D artists.

As of this writing, 3D graphics is rapidly expanding into the world of print, video, and multimedia. Inexpensive color printing, desktop video editing, and fast, affordable Macintosh computers have vaulted 3D in general, and Infini-D in particular, into the mainstream graphic arts community. You've probably noticed it yourself; everywhere you look you see flying chrome logos or gorgeous interactive 3D games. From television to multimedia, CD-ROMs to print advertisement, 3D graphics is adding depth, style, pizzazz, and breathing life into people's artistic visions.

FIGURE **1.1**

"Gallery" ©1995 by Daniel Sroka, Specular Int'l

FIGURE **1.2**

"Cabinet" ©1995 by Daniel Underhill, White Space Design

3D graphics and animation are being used in a spectrum of different situations for a variety of purposes. One example is product visualization. In the past, artists had to sketch pictures or even build physical models of new ideas for product packaging. Infini-D, combined with Photoshop, enables artists to create full-blown 3D renderings of their product concepts in brilliant 3D color, usually within an afternoon. Also, using alpha channels, Infini-D renderings can be composited onto a scanned image of a shelf with other products so that the client can see how the new packaging fits in with existing products.

FIGURE 1.3

"Cobble Street" ©1995 by Jen Jeneral and David Merck, Specular Int'l

Another rapidly growing use of 3D graphics is in multimedia production. Full-fledged games, such as *Jewels of the Oracle* and *Journeyman Project II: Buried in Time,* used Infini-D to create stunning 3D worlds. The advantage of 3D graphics in a medium such as this is that, after a 3D environment has been modeled, there are limitless angles, fly-throughs, and pans that can be created simply by moving Infini-D's 3D cameras. This enables artists to create a multimedia experience where viewers can "walk through" and interact with a 3D world molded entirely from the imagination of the creator.

3D graphics also are being integrated with traditional digital graphic arts tools, such as Illustrator, FreeHand, and Photoshop. It is simple to import an EPS logo from Illustrator or FreeHand into Infini-D, turn it into a 3D extrusion, add surfaces such as metal, marble, or wood, and composite it against a background in Photoshop. Small details such as bevels and specular highlights add uncanny realism to these logos, and give them a modern, attractive look.

FIGURE 1.4

"Gatorade Cans" © by Robert Drummond, MLR & Associates

Finally, 3D graphics are appearing with increasing frequency on television and digital video productions. If you watch television, you must have seen chrome or gold flying logos, such as during the introduction to a football game or the beginning of a news show. Type 1 or TrueType fonts can be turned into 3D type or combined with EPS logos within Infini-D. Using alpha channels, animation easily can be composited onto backgrounds using programs such as Adobe Premiere or Avid Videoshop.

As of this writing, 3D graphics are beginning to appear on the World Wide Web. New standards, such as VRML (Virtual Reality Modeling Language) and 3DMF (QuickDraw3D Metafile), enable artists to use 3D data in their Web pages. 3D information is much more compact than GIF and JPEG graphics and offers Web surfers an interactive experience, enabling them to "walk through" a 3D environment. This functionality, combined with an explosion in the availability of inexpensive 3D accelerators, promises to add a limitless supply of 3D images to the World Wide Web that can be explored with the click of a mouse.

FIGURE 1.7

"Knowledge Dream" ©1995 by
Javier Roca, Specular Int'l

FIGURE 1.8

"Earth 2" by Dream Quest Images,
©1995 Amblin Television &
Universal Television

FIGURE 1.9

"Three Views of a Blimp" ©*1995 by Tim Landry*

Infini-D: Class Project to World-Class Product

Many Infini-D users are unaware of the product's humble beginnings. Infini-D started as a class project at the University of Massachusetts between Adam Lavine and Dennis Chen, the founders of Specular. The class, ECE 660 taught by Sandy Hill, focused on 3D graphics, specifically ray tracing. (See Appendix C for information on Sandy Hill's textbook) Adam and Dennis worked to create a ray tracer with a usable interface, and eventually began to add animation and modeling controls. When it became clear that ray tracing was unsuitable for animation work due to lengthy rendering times, Adam and Dennis added a *shader*, or the capability to shade individual polygons, that dramatically decreased rendering times.

Before long, Adam and Dennis realized that they had a viable product on their hands. In the summer of 1990, Adam and Dennis were joined by Damian Roskill (now a rapper), Andrei Herasimchuk (now with Adobe), Dave Cotter (also with Adobe), and Carolyn Davis (still with Specular). Together, they founded Specular and decided to make a go of it in the Macintosh software market.

Infini-D 1.0, released in April of 1991, had a shader, ray tracer, and an event-based animation sequencer that enabled a great deal of flexibility in creating animation. Before Infini-D, most Macintosh 3D animation software was *keyframe-based*, meaning that users had to put in a separate keyframe for each stage of motion and *tween*, or in-between, the different keyframes. This technique had many problems. The animator had to think in terms of frames, not time, and making changes to a scripted animation was time-consuming and difficult. Infini-D's event-based sequencer, still in use today, enables users to change the timing, sequence, and character of their animation simply by dragging these events.

Alas, Infini-D 1.0 had its flaws. The biggest problem was the lack of text tools or support for EPS import. Infini-D 1.0 users had to create text or logos by drawing them in the Workshop! Infini-D 1.1 added support for TrueType fonts, and some clever users found ways to import EPS logos by creating an artificial font, using Fontographer and Illustrator, that enabled them to type their logo into Infini-D.

Infini-D 2.0 was a huge jump forward. Not only did Infini-D 2.0 add support for EPS and Type1 fonts, but Specular also overhauled the rendering engine, adding broadcast quality anti-aliasing and alpha channel support. When David Biedny, well-known Photoshop guru and sharp-eyed pixel watcher, reviewed Infini-D 2.0 in MacUser, he ran the rendered images by his friend, Photoshop author, and ILM special effects artist, John Knoll. They were so impressed by the jump in visual quality offered in Infini-D 2.0 that they gave Infini-D the coveted Five-Mouse rating!

Infini-D Today

Today, Infini-D 3.0 is a completely new program. It has support for splines in the Workshop, enabling users to import EPS logos and edit the curves. Animation control has been vastly improved with advanced animation features, such as onscreen motion paths and velocity graphs that rival high-end workstations in control over precise, professional motion. Rendering features, such as alpha texture mapping, gels, and masks for lights, have been added. Because Infini-D is Power Macintosh native, it offers blazing rendering speeds on Power Macintosh computers and PowerPC-based Macintosh-compatible computers.

Infini-D 3.1, shipping around the time this book hits the street, adds support for QuickDraw 3D, which dramatically enhances the interactive, 3D experience. Version 3.1 also provides more control over QuickTime movie texture mapping and offers enhanced texture map drag-and-drop support.

Infini-D has come a long way since April of 1991. It is used by tens of thousands of people worldwide to create a dazzling variety of 3D images and animation. It is rapidly becoming a staple in the graphics artist's arsenal of products, and has been at the top of the Macintosh graphic software bestseller's list since 1995. The vision of the early Infini-D, making 3D graphics powerful yet accessible, lives on within the product today. As you begin or continue your Infini-D experience, you will find that a great deal of power is lurking under the hood that enables you to express your ideas and imagination with greater ease than you ever dreamed possible.

Infini-D Basics

Infini-D is known for its simple, easy-to-use interface. As with any program, however, there are some basics to learn. Infini-D is designed so that these basics are easy to grasp. Tools are modeled after familiar tools from other programs, and interface elements are designed to be simple and logical. As you begin to explore the program, more power and functionality will unfold. Before long, Infini-D becomes a powerful, useful, and *still* easy-to-use graphics package. Infini-D is ideal for users at all levels of experience. This chapter explains Infini-D basics and introduces some tips for using those basic elements.

The World/Modeler Relationship

FIGURE 2.1

The Top View of the Infini-D world presents a bird's eye view that lets artists see a map-like representation of their scene.

FIGURE 2.2
The Camera View looks into the World through the lens of the camera. The Camera View is in three dimensions and can be edited to any angle or position, thus giving the artist complete control of the view into a scene.

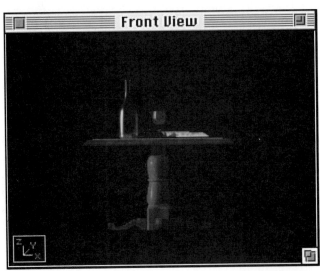

FIGURE 2.3

A front view of the scene is available in the Front View window.

FIGURE 2.4

The Right View looks at the scene from the side, giving artists a look at the depth angle of their work.

Before diving into the tools and functions of Infini-D, it's important to understand the metaphor that Infini-D uses. When you launch the program, four windows appear onscreen. These are your views into the *World* in which you work. Models are placed, animated, and rendered in these windows. Models, however, cannot be edited in the World. Just as you wouldn't build a table in your kitchen, nor a ship in the water, you don't build models in the Infini-D World. Modeling is done in a separate part of Infini-D, appropriately named the *Workshop*.

There are a couple of advantages to having a separate modeling space. First, this enables you to look at the model you're working on without the distraction of the rest of your scene. With only a few objects it might seem unnecessary to switch to another window, but, as your scenes get more complex, the advantages of a separate workshop become much more apparent.

Second, the Workshop enables you to have a separate toolbox designed specifically for building objects. A landscaper and a carpenter require different tools. If you follow the Infini-D metaphor, the landscaper designs the landscape, or scene, using appropriate landscaping tools. The carpenter, who builds objects in the workshop, uses object-building tools. When you switch into the Infini-D Workshop, the World toolbox is replaced by a set of drawing tools that help build and manipulate models.

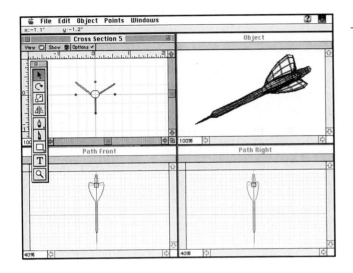

FIGURE 2.5

The Freeform layout is one of a number of possible workshop layouts. Creating new Workshop layouts is as simple as arranging Workshop windows and choosing Save from the Windows menu.

The Infini-D 3 Toolbox

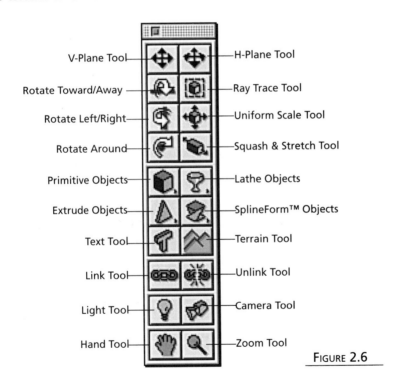

V-Plane Tool	H-Plane Tool
Rotate Toward/Away	Ray Trace Tool
Rotate Left/Right	Uniform Scale Tool
Rotate Around	Squash & Stretch Tool
Primitive Objects	Lathe Objects
Extrude Objects	SplineForm™ Objects
Text Tool	Terrain Tool
Link Tool	Unlink Tool
Light Tool	Camera Tool
Hand Tool	Zoom Tool

FIGURE 2.6

The Toolbox is your control panel for the Infini-D World. The *Infini-D Users Manual* explains the different tools in-depth, so this section will not review that material. Instead, this section focuses on where, when, and why to use particular tools, and how they can help make your work more productive. There have been considerable changes in the Toolbox since version 2.6, so it's worth looking at closely even if you're a veteran Infini-D user.

V-Plane and H-Plane Tools

The first two tools are the **V-Plane tool** and the **H-Plane tool**. V-Plane is the more common one; it acts as the arrow cursor into your virtual world. Infini-D's control-toggling facility provides a simple method to switch from tool to tool. Pressing the *Control key* almost always toggles back to the V-Plane tool from the current tool. This is a temporary toggle and releasing the Control key switches back to the last selected tool. Jumping to the V-Plane tool from another tool with a single key press is surprisingly useful. It saves immeasurable mouse travel when you're trying to make small adjustments to the position, scale, or rotation of an object.

> **TIP**
>
> Animation is simplified by Command key toggling. Press ⌘-M to take a snapshot, and adjust the next event in the animation without grabbing another tool.

Centerpoints

If you already have the V-Plane or H-Plane tool selected, holding the Control key enables you to move the centerpoint of an object. The centerpoint is the center of rotation and scaling. By moving the centerpoint, objects can be made to rotate around different axes, simplifying the creation of joints and hinges, or scaled in a specific direction, enabling objects to grow from a specific point or side. Chapter 9, "Importing 3D Objects," discusses centerpoints in more detail.

Modifier Keys

As with all standard Macintosh applications, holding the Shift key while dragging with the V- or H-Plane tools constrains the movement to a single axis. Normally, there are only two axes: vertical and horizontal. In Infini-D, however, you also can move along the depth axis because you're working in a three-dimensional world. Infini-D moves the object along the axis perpendicular to the face of the object you click. So, if you hold Shift and click the left side of an object, that object is temporarily limited to moving left or right.

The Option key also works in Infini-D as in other Macintosh-standard applications. If you hold the Option key and drag an object, a copy of the object is created and moved, leaving the original intact and unmoved.

Combinations of modifier keys can make the Infini-D Toolbox even more powerful. You can create grids, for example, by holding down the Shift and Option keys to constrain objects as you duplicate them.

Creating a Grid of Cubes

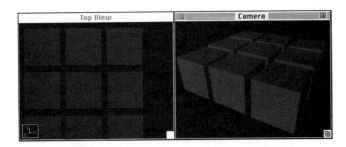

FIGURE 2.7
A cube grid

1. **Place a cube in the upper left corner of the Top View window.** This is the corner of the grid. It will be duplicated to create the rest of the grid.

2. **In the Camera View, press the Shift and Option keys, and drag the right side of** the cube. A copy of the cube drags away from the original. Repeat this step once more. You can watch the Top View while you're dragging the cubes to line them up. Or, the cubes can be placed and then aligned numerically using the *Object Floater*.

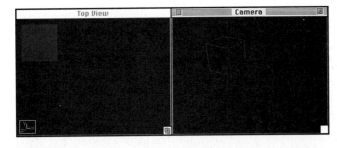

FIGURE 2.8
Start with a single cube.

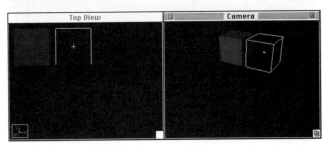

FIGURE 2.9
Define one side of the grid.

3. **With the Shift and Option keys still pressed, drag the left side of the original cube.** The cubes duplicate along another axis. Repeat this, and then drag copies of the first set of cubes.

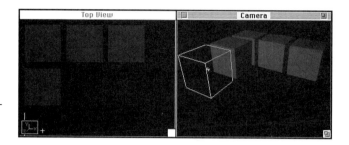

FIGURE 2.10

Fill in the second dimension of the grid.

Remember that the Infini-D world is not limited to working in a single plane. The cubes can be dragged up or down to make grids at different angles or with more dimensions.

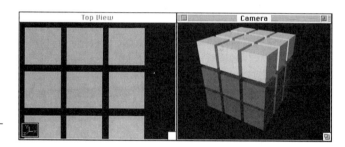

FIGURE 2.11

Add more dimensions.

Command Key

When your scenes get complicated, the *Command key* (⌘) should become one of the most-used modifier keys. Holding the Command key down while clicking in a scene brings up a menu of all the objects at that point. That is, holding the Command key down while clicking displays a list of all objects overlapping at the cursor position. Because the Infini-D world is three-dimensional, objects can be hidden behind other objects, making them difficult, if not impossible, to select. With the Command key, you can select any object no matter how many objects are in front of it.

Rotation Tools

The Rotation tools are affected by the same modifier keys as the Movement tools, but with quite different results in some cases. Shift and Option still follow the Mac standard: Shift constrains rotation to the axis perpendicular to the selected face, and Option duplicates objects from the original object. The Command key, however, has a completely different result. Pressing the Command key turns any of the three Rotation tools into a *virtual trackball*, enabling rotation in any direction.

Inside Infini-D: Using The Virtual Trackball

Here's how the *virtual trackball* works: when you click an object with the Free Rotate tool (⌘ + any Rotate tool), Infini-D creates an invisible circle around the centerpoint of the object. You can see the circle in the Workshop whenever you rotate anything in the Object view. If you keep the cursor inside the circle, Infini-D will rotate the object as if around a trackball, moving in the general direction of the cursor movement. Outside of the circle, the object spins around an axis perpendicular to your current view.

The trackball enables you to maneuver objects quickly. You can use the normal Rotate tools and the Object Floater to align objects more precisely after you've placed and oriented them using the trackball.

There are a few other modifier key combinations that are useful to know, but which require more explanation. They'll be discussed later in the book.

Ray Tracing

Before we move on to navigation, there is one oddball tool near the top of the Toolbox: the **Ray Trace tool**. The Ray Trace tool defines a small rectangle and ray traces that section of the image. It's always good to know what the final image will look like before doing your final rendering, and the Ray Trace tool enables you to do just that. You can check details and monitor small parts of your scene without waiting through the process of rendering the entire scene. To take that one step further, holding the Option key down changes the tool from a rectangular marquee to a lasso, enabling you to define arbitrary shapes to ray trace. Learn to use the Ray Trace tool effectively, and you'll save yourself a lot of rendering time. It's never fun to a render scene for an hour or more only to find mistakes to be fixed or tweaks to be made.

FIGURE 2.12

The virtual trackball is the default Rotation tool in the Workshop. When used, the cursor changes to indicate the mode of rotation and a circle appears to show the rotation regions.

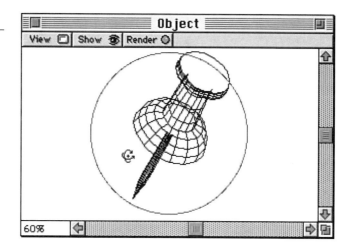

Ray tracing is a rendering technique that tracks the path of light from the source to an object. It accurately depicts color and intensity of light as well as reflections. It is sometimes referred to as *photorealistic*.

Navigation

Navigation in the Infini-D 3 World has evolved considerably. The navigation panel from earlier versions has been replaced completely with new tools, which enable you to move faster and more intuitively. There are, however, some significant differences between moving the standard views and moving the camera. Let's start with the new *Zoom tool.*

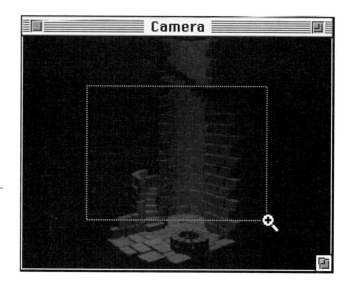

FIGURE 2.13

The Zoom tool is a magnifying glass. By clicking and dragging with the Zoom tool, you define a rectangle that Infini-D magnifies to fill the window.

The Zoom tool is used to zoom in and out of the standard views. Normally, the tool zooms in on a view, but by holding the Option key, you can make it zoom out. Also note that if you click and drag to define a rectangle using the Zoom tool, Infini-D makes that rectangle fill the entire window. To reset the view, simply double-click the Zoom tool. The window resets to the default magnification and centers the view. With the latter two functions, you can zoom in on specific parts of your scene, examine them up close, and then reset the view to see the larger picture. Combined with the Ray Trace tool, no details should be missed before rendering the final image or animation.

In the Camera window, the Zoom tool is functionally the same. Be careful, though. *The camera object is not moved by the Zoom tool.* The camera's lens is affected instead, just like a telephoto lens on a real camera. In print, this might seem natural, but be aware of the difference between moving a camera and zooming a camera. When a camera zooms, the position stays the same so the perspective cannot change. The image gets larger or smaller, but the perspective stays at the camera's location. As a result, the image can be distorted.

Object Lesson: Use Lens Distortion for Special Effects

You can use camera lens distortion to create effects, such as a fisheye lens.

1. **Zoom the camera out** or use a preset camera lens from the Edit Current View dialog in the Render menu. There's a specific fisheye lens setting, or you can make a custom lens setting.

2. **Move the camera in close to your objects.** Make sure to move the camera object itself, either by moving the camera object or using the Hand tool. The closer you get, the more the perspective distorts, replicating the effect of a fisheye camera lens or a peephole in a door. Don't get too close, however, or your objects are clipped. That is, the objects are so close to the lens that the camera can't see them, and holes appear on the front faces. If you see the front corners of your objects disappearing, move the camera back a little.

FIGURE 2.14

A fisheye lens effect is created by adjusting the focal length of the camera using the Zoom tool or via the View Info dialog.

Pressing ⌘-Spacebar brings up the Zoom-in tool, and adding the Option key to that combination zooms out.

Hand Tool

The Hand tool works like you would expect it to in any Macintosh application. You can access the Hand tool with the Spacebar and use it to drag the view like you would a piece of paper. That is, click and drag the view to the left and the view moves to the left as if the hand were actually grabbing and holding the scene. This is true for all views.

In the Camera view, the Hand tool has several other capabilities. Holding the ⌘ key enables left-right rotation of the camera object itself. ⌘-Shift rotates the camera up and down and ⌘-Option makes the camera roll. Using these key combinations, you can point the camera in any direction, without running back and forth to the Toolbox. If that seems a little confusing at first, try zooming out of one of the standard views so the camera's movement is visible. Watch how the rotation affects the direction the camera points. Also, don't hesitate to grab the camera object in another view and rotate it using the Rotation tools or the trackball discussed previously.

To move the camera in and out, press and hold the Option key. The camera object is moved instead of just zooming the lens. That way perspective is preserved, and your scenes will not distort.

All the different modifier keys can be confusing, so it's a good idea to keep the Infini-D Reference Card handy until you know the different options.

QuickDraw 3D

With the release of Infini-D version 3.1, Specular added support for Apple's *QuickDraw 3D* technology. QuickDraw 3D is supported only on the Power Macintosh, so if you're running a Macintosh based on a 680x0 (68K) processor, you won't have access to these features. 68K users will not lose any other features, however, because no other options are Power Mac dependent. With a PowerPC processor, the QuickDraw 3D extensions, and version 3.1 of Infini-D you have an extremely powerful system that enables you to work quickly and visually, with shaded feedback in any view. If you don't have that Power Mac yet, but were thinking of upgrading, QuickDraw 3D is an excellent reason to do so.

QuickDraw 3D is a real time, system-level rendering engine. Part of the package is a model format called *3DMF*. Having a system-level engine and a file format means objects can be treated as PICT files or text files would be. Models can be moved between applications supporting the format via cut and paste, stored in the Scrapbook, and easily exchanged with other computers, even on different platforms. Infini-D even supports Macintosh drag-and-drop, which lets you drag objects directly into other applications.

The speed that QuickDraw 3D provides can change the way you work. The capability to see models with shaded surfaces while building, arranging, and animating them virtually eliminates all of the guesswork. The interaction of the Workshop and the World has increased dramatically, making the modeling, animation, and rendering processes much quicker, easier, and more enjoyable.

FIGURE 2.15
QuickDraw 3D enables fast and better shading for any view.

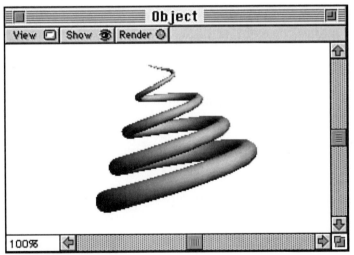

FIGURE 2.16
QuickDraw 3D adds shading capabilities to the workshop, enabling artists to see models shaded during construction.

The Productive Artist

3

In today's highly competitive graphics software market, many programs share a common affliction. While trying to be the most powerful, creativity-inducing product on the market, many programs lose usability and consequently slow down the artist's work. Apple Computer recently ran an advertising campaign that said, "It's not how powerful the computer is. It's how powerful the computer makes you." Not only is Apple's claim true for their computers, it is also true for the software that runs *on* their computers. Infini-D stands out in the 3D graphics market as a powerful program that helps its users to be productive. This chapter explains everything you need to know to fully exploit Infini-D's power and maintain optimal productivity.

Working Smart

In any program, there are optimal operating conditions. Infini-D is flexible enough to work well in many environments, but it has its own preferred system set-ups. The recommendations on the side of the software box and in the manual are often minimal configurations and should be used only as a basis on which to build.

RAM Requirements and Trade-offs

As you've probably guessed, the more RAM you have, the happier Infini-D will be. Especially with the large RAM requirements of the

Power Macintosh, Infini-D needs a reasonably large space and will let you know if it's feeling cramped. If you don't have a lot of RAM, don't lose hope. Here are a few tips for deciding how much RAM you're going to need and how much to allocate to the Infini-D application:

◆ **The minimum memory requirement for Infini-D is 6,000KB,** or a little bit less than 6MB of RAM. This means that you need at least 12MB total in your system. While that amount of RAM should be sufficient for small scenes on a 68K-based machine, it's a little low for a Power Mac. A good base to work with on a Power Mac is 16MB. With only 16MB, however, scene size is limited by the number of objects and imagemaps that

can be loaded. If possible, get 24MB to 32MB of RAM. This leaves plenty of room for scenes to grow, as well as for model complexity to increase.

◆ **Don't allocate all of your free RAM to Infini-D.** QuickTime usually loads when Infini-D loads. Giving all available RAM to Infini-D leaves none for the QuickTime extensions. QuickTime is required to run Infini-D on a Power Mac, so it is extremely important to leave space. QuickDraw 3D also needs space to load, if you're using a Power Macintosh. Usually, leaving 2MB free is enough room for the system to breathe and Infini-D to load, but with QuickDraw 3D, leave three or four megabytes free.

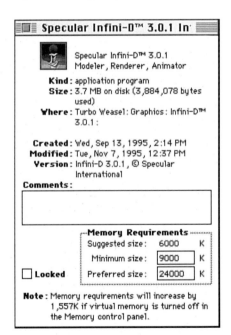

FIGURE 3.1

Infini-D's memory partition can be changed from the Finder by selecting the Infini-D icon and choosing Get Info from the File menu. The suggested size represents Infini-D's absolute minimum memory partition.

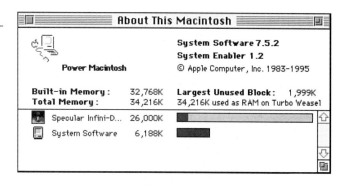

FIGURE 3.2

About This Macintosh in the Finder's Apple Menu displays currently running applications and their memory usage. Notice that almost two megabytes have been left free for QuickTime to load and the system to grow. If QuickDraw 3D needs to load, leave a couple more megabytes free.

♦ **Nothing beats real RAM.** The system's virtual memory and third-party RAM extension programs, such as RAM Doubler, give you more memory, but it's not the same as real RAM. While virtual memory works, there is significant loss in performance. In most cases, this loss is too great to work with effectively. Third-party memory extensions can cause problems with Infini-D's memory management and are usually not recommended. There is one exception to the virtual memory rule: On Power Macintosh computers, the memory management scheme is set up such that having virtual memory on significantly decreases the memory requirements of Power Mac native applications. To take advantage of the decreased memory requirements that virtual memory can provide, turn virtual memory on at the minimum expansion setting, one megabyte more than the real RAM in your system. This decreases Infini-D's memory requirements by nearly two megabytes without severely affecting performance.

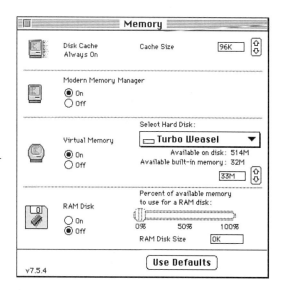

FIGURE 3.3

The Memory control panel houses the controls for virtual memory. Here virtual memory has been set to expand memory by only one megabyte to take advantage of lower RAM requirements without hampering speed.

◆ **Make sure there is free space on your hard drive.** If Infini-D needs to, it can create virtual memory files of its own. Without space on the hard disk, not only is there a problem finding space to render your final images and animation, but Infini-D won't have any place to store temporary files. Real RAM is still better, though, and Infini-D is faster if it doesn't have to store anything on the hard drive.

◆ **Close unnecessary windows when not in use.** Every open window requires a space in RAM. When you close windows that aren't in use, RAM can be allocated to other processes. Also, the larger the window, the more RAM required. An efficient method of working with Infini-D's many-windowed world is to set up the scene with the necessary windows, and then, when the scene is finished, close all windows except the window to be rendered (probably the Camera window). During rendering, all free RAM is allocated to the one window instead of sharing it between several windows.

◆ **The more RAM you have, the faster Infini-D will go.** This is the basic trade-off. Infini-D works fastest in RAM, and the more you have, the faster it will go. The speed is limited, of course, by what the processor can handle and how large the scene is. Adding a lot of RAM to a Quadra will not make it as fast as a Power Mac, but it will improve performance significantly. Also, if a scene can be stored entirely in RAM, adding more will have little effect.

Camera Use and Setup

Cameras are the basic eyes of Infini-D. Cameras can be moved and animated, they show perspective, and you can have multiple, unique cameras. By contrast, the View windows cannot be rotated and are orthographic, meaning there is no perspective. View windows are two-dimensional views of the scene, while cameras are three-dimensional and can move around freely.

Camera use is fairly simple. There are only a few basics to remember.

FIGURE **3.4**

Infini-D supports multiple cameras, which display unique views.

◆ **Try not to resize cameras.** Infini-D enables cameras to be scaled up and down to make them easier to work with in the view windows. Despite this capability, however, rendering images through the lens of a scaled camera can cause undesired effects. A large camera's view is no larger than a small camera's view. Making a camera larger will not change the view at all. In fact, if the camera object is scaled, the camera view will not even redraw. However, because of the large scale, to get close-up views of objects, the camera must be moved so near that it begins to envelop the objects. While this is not inherently a problem, it can cause confusion. Objects are sometimes clipped by being too close to the camera. If it becomes necessary to scale the camera in order to select and move it, scale the camera, move and rotate as desired, and then scale it back down. At the normal size, minor adjustments can be made using the Navigation tools or the Object Floater.

◆ **Use Bookmarks liberally.** If you see any view of your scene that looks good, just press the + button on the Views Floater. That view is then available at any time, simply by selecting it from the Bookmark pop-up on the Views Floater. When a good camera angle happens, save it. It is difficult to get exactly the same angle and position again. Later, if you decide you don't need that camera position any more, selecting the bookmark and pressing the – button will delete it.

FIGURE 3.5

This is what happens when you put your head through the lens of a camera. Clipping occurs when objects are too close to the camera, a problem with large cameras. Smaller cameras are more maneuverable and less likely to collide with other objects.

FIGURE 3.6

Bookmarks are listed at the bottom of the Views Floater.

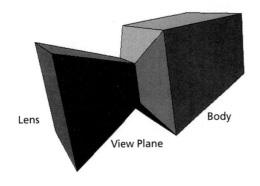

Lens

View Plane

Body

FIGURE **3.7**

The Infini-D camera is comprised of two parts: the body and the lens. The view plane occurs at the intersection of the two parts.

NOTE

Inside Infini-D: How Infini-D's Cameras "See."

Each camera has something inside it called the view plane. The view plane is invisible to the user, but it is of fundamental use to the camera. The view plane is like a screen inside the camera where all images are drawn. That is, the camera window is a picture of exactly what the view plane sees. A camera object is made up of two parts: the body, which is the cube with a slanted bottom, and the lens, which is the pyramid-like cone on the front of the camera. The view plane exists at the point where the lens and the body of the camera meet. That's why objects can get close enough to a camera to be inside the lens, but get clipped as they move back into the body of the camera.

Working Quickly

One of the most difficult problems in any 3D package is working at a reasonable rate without waiting for the computer to catch up. It is important to see the scenes clearly each step of the way, but re-rendering a scene at final image quality takes too long to use frequently. Drawing scenes in wireframe is much faster, but gives less of a sense of what the scene looks like. This section introduces some techniques for working at a reasonable pace that won't sacrifice previews of the final images.

Wireframe Modes

When using Infini-D, you need to know what you're creating, but you can't spend the time waiting for the window to re-render for every little change. Wireframe is fast, but surfaces are only represented by the color of the wireframe, objects don't hide each other as they pass in front of one another, and sometimes it's difficult to see what's what, especially in a complex scene. Shading shows you most of what you need to see, but takes much longer, sometimes longer than you might want to wait.

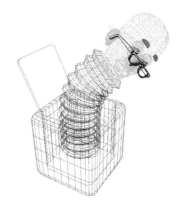

FIGURE 3.8

Wireframe mode shows objects as a framework of lines. Wireframe is fast, but shows little surface detail.

FIGURE 3.9

Patch detail, from left to right: low, medium, and high. Low detail has considerably fewer polygons than high and renders accordingly faster, but high provides much smoother curves in wireframe or shading modes.

Wireframe is a good mode for setting up your scene. You can usually get by with a rough sketch of the scene when you are just placing objects and moving them around. Wireframe detail is affected by the *patch detail* setting in the Preferences dialog. Setting the patch detail to high or medium will break the model into many polygons, making smoother curves and more details. For faster work, set the patch details to low. Fewer polygons means less work for Infini-D.

TIP

Wireframe is not the only thing affected by patch detail setting. Shading modes reflect the change as well. Try working in low patch detail whether in wireframe or a shaded

mode. When you render the final images, switch back to medium or high patch detail. Rendering slows down, but the quality improves. If your final images are ray traced, work in low patch detail, but don't worry about the patch detail setting when you render. Ray tracing ignores the patch detail and uses splines to create smooth curves and edges.

If there are a lot of objects, try using wireframe Draft Mode. Draft Mode draws the rails and cross sections instead of breaking the model into polygons. This is a faster method, but doesn't show as much detail. Work in Draft Mode to do set up, and switch to a higher drawing setting when you need more accuracy.

FIGURE 3.10

Draft Mode is an ultra-low patch detail mode that only affects wireframe. In fact, Draft Mode displays the shape the ray tracer will render. Thus, Draft Mode can be used to get a quick, surface-less preview of an object's shape when ray traced.

QuickDraw 3D

Apple's QuickDraw 3D is the quickest way to work. QuickDraw 3D enables Infini-D to draw and animate objects with shaded surfaces in real time. Thus, there is no guessing at what scenes will look like, or how smoothly animation will play. Additionally, QuickDraw 3D supports hardware acceleration. For a small investment, an accelerator will dramatically improve QuickDraw 3D's already impressive speed.

There's little more to say to express the advantages of the QuickDraw 3D environment. It is the fastest way to work and gives excellent feedback. *One word of warning, though: QuickDraw 3D requires a good deal of RAM. It will not run in less than 16 megabytes of RAM, and more is necessary to create scenes of any complexity.*

Scene Size

As scene sizes grow, Infini-D deals with more and more information. Consequently, the larger the scene, the slower Infini-D goes. The effects of this slowdown might not be immediately visible, given a fast machine with a good amount of RAM, but eventually even the fastest computer will feel the squeeze and slow down.

A good solution to the over-sized scene problem is to break the scene into several files. For example, suppose you have an animation moving from the outside of a building to a room inside of the building. The animation *could* be created as a single scene containing both the inside and outside of the building. However, the inside of the building could be moved to a separate scene, thereby easing Infini-D's workload and speeding up the program. Here's how to create a scene and divide it into separate files.

1. **Create all models in one scene.** By creating models in a single space, scale can be maintained and positioning objects is easier. Keeping all objects uniformly scaled and lined up greatly simplifies the process of later rejoining the final rendered animation.

FIGURE 3.11

By creating all models in one scene, scale and position can be maintained for easier rejoining after rendering.

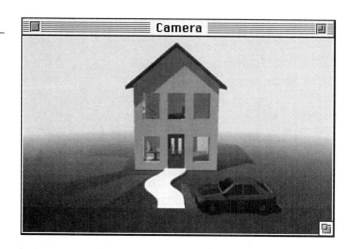

2. **Copy and paste a section of the scene into a new file.** In the example above, the room inside the building might be linked to a single parent object. By copying and pasting that single object, the whole room is easily moved from one scene to another. See Chapter 10, "Animation," for more information on linking objects. Alternatively, save the first scene and duplicate it in the Finder. Then, open the duplicated scene and delete unnecessary objects.

3. **Animate the first scene.** By animating the outside of the building first, the camera's end position can be moved to the second file; thus, a starting point is created that blends smoothly when the animations are joined. You might also need to copy some object locations, rotations, or scales if any objects are animated.

FIGURE 3.12

All objects outside of the house's first floor were deleted, because they are not visible when the camera is inside the house.

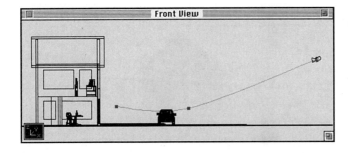

FIGURE 3.13

Create the animation in the first scene to create the initial camera position for the second scene.

4. **Copy and paste the camera from the first scene to the second.** This creates the starting point for the animation in the second scene.

5. **Delete any unnecessary camera animation events.** In most cases, the last event is the only relevant event, because earlier animation occurs in the other scene. You might, however, find it useful to render some overlapping animation. By doing so, you gain some freedom in how the two animations align. Without overlap, the two scenes must match correctly on a single frame.

6. **Animate the second scene.** With the end point of the first scene exactly lined up with the starting point of the second, and with all objects' positions lined up from one scene to the next, animations rendered from the two scenes should be joined.

After both scenes are animated, it's a good idea to check the velocity graphs of moving objects to make sure the velocities are the same where the two animations will be joined. That way the animation is smooth through the two files.

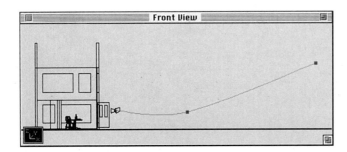

FIGURE 3.14

Move the camera and its animation events to the second scene for reference to camera positions in the first scene.

FIGURE 3.15

The eventmarks from the first scene are deleted, leaving only the last event as the starting position for the second scene.

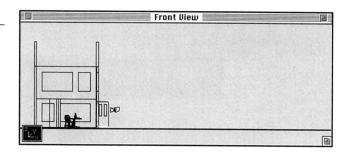

FIGURE 3.16

Animate the second scene without the added workload of the first scene to slow you down.

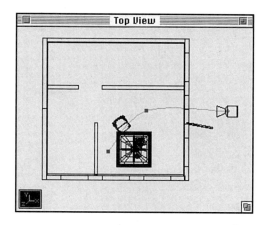

Experiment with different ways to show and hide objects that are visible from both scenes. In this scene, the camera flies in the door of the building. As the camera approaches the window, the room inside should be visible. Part of the outside of the building has been copied to the second scene along with the room. The animation in the first scene, outside of the building, only needs to get close enough to the building so that the front of the building fills the window. As long as the rest of the outside view is not visible, the scene can switch with no noticeable change. In this case, use the last camera event of the first scene for the first camera event in the second scene. Although overlap can be used if desired, it is not necessary.

join these two frames

first scene animation

second scene animation

FIGURE 3.17

After rendering, the two animations are merged by joining the two identical frames.

Birth and Death Events

A simpler, more elegant solution to the scene size problem is found in the Eventmark Info dialog. The checkbox labeled End Animation is used to indicate a *death event*. A death event indicates the end of an object's existence and is used to make objects disappear. Death, however, is not permanent for Infini-D models. By changing the dead object farther along the sequencer's timeline, a *birth event* is created, bringing the dead object back into existence.

Birth and death events are a much easier way to speed up rendering time. If an object is dead, it is not calculated during rendering. Thus, objects can simply be killed—or turned off—rather than copied and pasted into a new scene. Birth events enable you to bring objects back later, as well. Using the separate scene method would require a second scene switch to go back to the first scene.

The only drawback to death events is that hierarchically linked objects are not affected by a parent's death. That is, if two objects are linked and the parent object is killed, the child object is not killed. In this case, each object must be manually switched off.

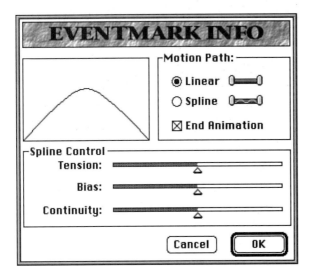

FIGURE 3.18

By checking the End Animation box, an eventmark becomes a death event, hiding the associated object until the next birth event.

Model Complexity

Infini-D 3 introduces a brand-new modeler, enabling the user to create much more complex objects. The new modeler creates objects that were not possible in the previous versions of Infini-D. This new, more powerful modeling environment is capable of building single object models that would have been built out of several objects in the old Infini-D workshops. That is, models that would have been made from several simpler objects in older versions of Infini-D can now be made as single, more complex objects. Single objects are easier to deal with from the user's point of view; there is only one object to manipulate instead of several, aligning and linking objects is not an issue, and models can be smoother because there are no joints between objects. While these are obvious benefits, there are some reasons to temper the use of single object models in place of multiple objects.

◆ **Animation can be more difficult.** When a model is made of several objects, the joints can act almost like hinges. Moving these small parts is as simple as rotating or moving them with the standard tools. Single objects, however, must be *morphed* to be animated. That is, the model must be brought back into the Workshop and edited to move any part of it. While morphing is suitable for many applications, such as bending a wine glass or bottle, achieving the movement desired in other situations, such as an arm bending or a box opening, can be much more difficult.

◆ **Applying surfaces to multiple objects is more accurate.** Placing surfaces on a single, complex object is certainly possible, and quite effective, but aligning several different surfaces on the same object can become unmanageable. By breaking the model into several pieces, surfaces can be applied to each object much more accurately.

FIGURE 3.19

The box on the left is a single object. The box on the right, a multiple object model, is animated much more easily.

FIGURE **3.20**

The lamp on the left is a single object with a decal surface. The lamp on the right is two objects, which enables much better control of surfaces as well as the use of mixed mode rendering for different surface effects.

◆ **Multiple object models can take advantage of Infini-D's movement constraining capabilities.** By linking and constraining object movement and rotation, multiple object models can be made to behave very much like their real-world counterparts. A ladder, for example, can be limited to extending a certain distance, or a stepladder could have a limited open angle.

A good rule of thumb for deciding when to break up a model and when to build a single object is this: consider the object being built. If, in the real world, the object is created out of a single piece, or is effectively used as a single piece, it is a good candidate for the single object model.

FIGURE **3.21**

These ladders demonstrate constraining. They are limited so that they extend and open like real ladders, simplifying the animation process.

A bottle, for example, is a single object. The handset on a phone is several objects joined indistinctly such that it becomes a single object for all practical purposes. On the other hand, if the real-world object is created out of several distinct parts, it probably should be constructed from those individual parts in Infini-D as well. The base of a telephone, for example, is made of many different parts. The buttons on the telephone's keypad are much easier to animate if each is a separate object, and the imagemaps for the numbers on the buttons are much simpler if a separate image can be assigned to each button, rather than attempting to align images for each of the buttons on a single object.

Primitives

Infini-D has a set of simple objects called *primitives*. These primitive objects are a cube, a sphere, a cylinder, a cone, a square, and an infinite plane. Although it might seem pointless to include such basic objects in a program with as powerful a modeler as Infini-D's, there is one major benefit to using primitives wherever possible.

Primitives are represented mathematically in Infini-D. That is, each object is represented by a simple mathematical formula that describes a simple shape. Using formulas results in greatly increased speed. A primitive cube always renders faster than an equivalent cube built in the

Workshop. Thus, if it is at all possible to represent objects or parts of objects using primitive shapes, rendering time will decrease noticeably.

Rendering Options with Infini-D: Flat vs. Gouraud vs. Phong vs. Ray Tracing

To use Infini-D in the most efficient way possible, it is important to understand the various rendering modes and options. Choosing the right rendering mode can significantly affect your rendering times, and often a faster rendering mode provides virtually identical results to a higher quality, more computationally expensive mode.

Fast shading

Fast shading, also known as *flat shading and Shade-Fast* in Infini-D, is used primarily as a previewing method, although for certain types of images and animation fast shading can suffice to get the job done. Fast shading fills every polygon or facet of the model with a distinct, uniform color; it's as if each polygon is filled with its own little paint bucket. Infini-D calculates the color at the exact center of the polygon and then fills the entire polygon with that color. This is much faster than Gouraud or Phong shading, which calculate the color of many pixels within the polygon, but fast shading does not create the amount of detail or realism as the higher quality rendering modes.

FIGURE 3.22

The six primitives in Infini-D are, from left to right, the cube, sphere, cylinder, cone, square, and, underneath the others, the infinite plane.

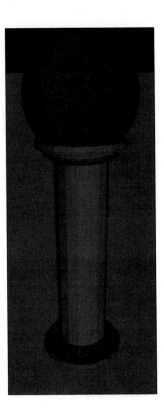

In general, fast shading does not have the high quality required for most final projects. However, you can save time on certain types of objects with flat faces that don't need a lot of detail, such as cubes, squares, and infinite planes. Also, if you need to create a rough, shaded animation or image to get an idea across, fast shading can be ideal.

Gouraud Shading

Gouraud shading, known as *Shade-Better* in Infini-D, is one notch up from fast shading in terms of quality, but also one notch down in terms of speed. Gouraud shading looks at the pixels at the corners of a polygon and interpolates, or smears, the colors between them. Gouraud shading often has a blurry or smudged look, especially with texture maps (scanned images). While this technique isn't useful for texture maps or procedural surfaces, such as marbles and woods, it works extremely well for creating chrome and gold type or logo effects, especially when combined with an environment map (see Chapter 6, "Setting the Mood: Environment and Lighting").

FIGURE 3.24

A Gouraud shaded column is smoother because the color is averaged and smoothed.

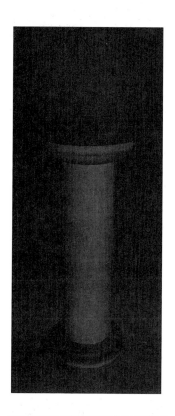

FIGURE 3.25

Using an environment map with Gouraud shading can create stunning gold or chrome effects.

Gouraud shading also can work if the object has a smooth surface, such as plastic, without a lot of light reflection or specular highlights. Additionally, you can get away with Gouraud shading if the object is small or in the background.

Phong Shading

Named after Bui-Tuong Phong, *Phong shading* samples every single pixel within a scene. Known as *Shade-Best* within Infini-D, Phong shading results in highly detailed texture and surface maps, offering a great deal of visual realism. This realism, however, comes at a price. Depending on the complexity of the scene and the surface maps, Phong Shading can take up to five times longer than Gouraud shading, and ten times longer than fast shading.

Phong shading is often used for final quality output because of its capability to render detailed surface maps. Infini-D also offers an option in Phong for shadows that further enhances the visual quality of the final image or animation. Ray tracing is sometimes required, because Phong shading does not support true reflections or transparencies. For most images and animation, however, Infini-D's Phong shading is sufficient for a professional-quality final image or animation.

Ray Tracing

Ray tracing is the most visually sophisticated and realistic of Infini-D's rendering options. And, in keeping with the Universal Principle of 3D Computer Graphics (*The better it looks, the longer it takes*), ray tracing is also the most computationally demanding rendering option available in Infini-D. This description of ray tracing is slightly longer than the descriptions of flat, Gouraud, and Phong shading, but an understanding of the principles of ray tracing enables you to better understand 3D computer graphics in general.

FIGURE **3.26**

With Phong shading, texture maps and procedural surfaces, such as the tile in this scene, are drawn.

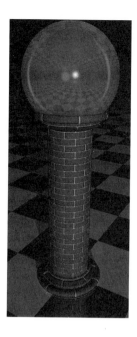

Light Reversed: In the real world, light is emitted from light sources, bounces off the various objects around us, and hits our eyes. A red ball sitting in the middle of a well-lit room absorbs all the light in the spectrum *except* red. The red light is reflected off the ball into our eyes, hence the ball's redness. In ray tracing, the phenomenon is reversed. Within your virtual world, beams or *rays* are emitted from your eye (in this case, an Infini-D camera) through every pixel on your screen. These rays bounce around your 3D world until they find a light, telling Infini-D how to color that pixel.

FIGURE 3.28

Two spheres above the Mona Lisa show ray tracing's true reflections and refractive transparency.

Reflection and Refraction: Rays bounce off reflective objects, and go through refractive—or transparent—objects. In figure 3.28, there are two spheres sitting on a scanned picture of the Mona Lisa, one mirrored and one transparent. Rays fired from the camera into the mirrored sphere bounce off the sphere and into the picture; this tells Infini-D that that particular point on the sphere should combine the surface properties of the sphere as well as the area the ray hits. Similarly, in the case of the refractive sphere, the ray is shot *through* the sphere and is bent depending on the sphere's index of refraction. The area of the picture the ray collides with after passing through the sphere is then combined with the transparent surface of the sphere. If the sphere is blue, then the blue would combine with the refracted area of the picture to look like blue glass. The coolest thing about transparency, with Infini-D's ray tracing, is that the index of refraction for transparent objects *matches* real-world indices of refraction. So, if you know that water's index of refraction is 1.33, you can create highly realistic images of water using ray tracing. (For a list of real-world indices of refraction, see Appendix A.)

Mixed Mode Shading

Shading can be specified on a per-object basis in Infini-D. While this does not apply to ray tracing, it can be very useful in shaded scenes. A scene, for example, might contain a flying gold logo, some texture mapped objects, and some objects in the background. The texture mapped objects must be Phong shaded, but the logo only needs Gouraud shading to look good. The background objects can be Gouraud shaded or even fast shaded, depending on the detail desired.

FIGURE 3.29

Three shading modes mixed: the strip of UPC symbols uses texture maps, so Phong shading is necessary; the Generi Co. text looks good with Gouraud shading; and the large UPC symbol in the rear is fast shaded because it has very little detail.

To set the shading mode, select an object and choose Object Info from the Object menu (⌘+I). At the bottom of the Object Info dialog, select the desired shading mode. In this case, set the flying logo to Gouraud, the background objects to whichever mode is most appropriate, and render the scene using Shade-Best. Any objects whose shading modes were not specified will be Phong shaded. The rest are Gouraud or fast shaded.

Anti-aliasing Levels

There are three levels of *anti-aliasing* inInfini-D: Low, Medium, and High. Anti-aliasing, also known as *super-sampling*, smoothes out jagged edges, or *jaggies*, by over-sampling the area that needs to be smoothed. *Over-sampling* means that Infini-D looks extra hard at the area in question. For example, instead of casting one ray per pixel, Infini-D subdivides each pixel into four quadrants, fires a ray into each quarter of the pixel, and averages the results. This takes longer, but it also results in a pixel that more accurately represents the scene.

Table 3.1 lists Infini-D anti-aliasing levels and their appropriate uses.

So, for the pixels that are being anti-aliased, low takes 4 times longer, medium 12 times longer, and high 20 times longer. These numbers, however, can be a little misleading, because not all pixels are anti-aliased.

When to Use Which Anti-aliasing Method

In general, VHS-quality video and screen-resolution QuickTime movies are fine with low anti-aliasing. An NTSC video signal naturally blurs and softens a computer-generated image, so that low-anti-aliasing often can provide a good quality final animation. Medium is often used for higher quality video environments, such as Beta SP or digital video, and also for medium-to high-resolution print. High anti-aliasing should only be used for print. It should be used sparingly, because a 20× oversample, though it looks nice, can slow ray tracing to glacial speeds.

TABLE 3.1

Anti-Aliasing Level	Oversampling Rate	Uses
Low	4× Over-sample	VHS video, screen-resolution, QuickTime
Medium	12× Over-sample	Beta/D1/D2 video, medium- to high-resolution print
High	20× Over-sample	High-resolution print, people with very fast Macs

FIGURE 3.30

No anti-aliasing leaves rough, pixelated edges.

FIGURE 3.31

Low anti-aliasing is good for video and screen resolution images. This level of anti-aliasing smoothes edges somewhat but leaves images slightly blurry.

FIGURE 3.32

Medium anti-aliasing smoothes edges and is sufficient for most higher resolution purposes.

FIGURE 3.33

High anti-aliasing makes beautifully smooth edges but slows rendering to a crawl. Save high anti-aliasing for high-resolution images.

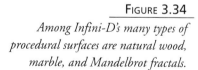

WORKING SMART

Only use the level of anti-aliasing you need to make your scene look clean and crisp. The goal is to get a good-looking final product quickly. It makes no sense to use high anti-aliasing if medium will be sufficient for your needs. Use the Rendering Options to choose an anti-aliasing mode for the Ray Trace tool, and render small patches of your scene to get an idea of what the final rendering will look like at a particular anti-aliasing level.

Procedural Surfaces vs. Digitized Texture Maps

A *procedural surface* is a computer-generated wood, marble, fractal, or noise surface. A *texture map* is a scanned or digitized picture that is wrapped around a 3D object. A procedural surface often can give you a unique look, but a digitized texture map gives you a wider variety of options and also renders much more quickly.

FIGURE 3.34

Among Infini-D's many types of procedural surfaces are natural wood, marble, and Mandelbrot fractals.

Procedural Surfaces

Infini-D generates wood, marble, and noise maps in three dimensions. That is, it generates a 3D texture out of which it carves your model. Because procedural surfaces are mathematically defined, you can morph between them to have swirling woods, morphing marbles, or zooming fractals. You also can join 3D objects together and, by selecting Use Parent Surface, tell Infini-D to carve them out of the same chunk of 3D matter, so that the surface is smooth and constant. You can even move an object through the 3D space of the procedural surface; you can define a block of marble and then move a vase through it! The downside is that procedural surfaces take longer to render than digitized texture maps, because each point on the surface must be calculated.

Texture Maps

Texture maps, usually PICT files, are a fast way to get good-looking results out of Infini-D. Texture maps also link your copy of Infini-D with Photoshop, dramatically leveraging the power of these applications. You can use digitized textures not only for the surfaces of objects, but also for the characteristics of their transparency, reflection, specular highlights, and bumpiness. You can also use alpha channels for decals (see section later in this chapter on alpha channels) and combine multiple texture maps on a single object for dramatic and interesting effects. The downside of texture maps is that they require more memory and disk space, and are not resolution-independent like procedural surfaces. The big upside is that there are a lot of them. Your scanner or a few CD-ROMS of good texture maps can provide a virtually infinite variety of interesting surfaces for your 3D artwork.

WORKING SMART

In general, texture maps are preferable to procedural surfaces, unless there is a specific effect you want to use. Wraptures™ Volumes I and II, for example, are an excellent starting point. You also can easily create your own texture maps with Adobe Photoshop, Fractal Painter, Kai's Power Tools, or Specular TextureScape. If you are going to use a procedural surface, remember that noise maps are fastest, woods are second fastest, and marbles are the slowest.

FIGURE 3.35

Any PICT or QuickTime movie can be imported into Infini-D and used as a surface.

Texture Map Sizes

It's often confusing to know how big texture maps should be. If you make them too big, they take up an inordinate amount of memory. If you make them too small, your surfaces can look jaggy or pixelized. Further, if you render your scene at high resolutions, your texture maps can quickly become too small, like painting a picture on a balloon and filling it with air.

Here's a good rule of thumb to make sure your texture map is the proper size: make sure the size and/or resolution matches the amount of screen or print space the portion of your 3D rendering uses. In other words, if you are wrapping a wood texture onto a wall that takes up 25 percent of a 1,000 × 1,000 pixel print image, make sure your wood texture is at least 250 × 250. If you want to be extra safe, you can match the texture maps with the size of your final output from Infini-D, but this takes more memory and disk space (Infini-D uses a disk caching setup for texture maps).

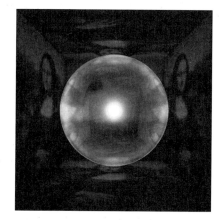

FIGURE 3.36

In this picture, the Mona Lisa is too small. As a result, the image is blurry and difficult to see.

FIGURE 3.37

This Mona Lisa image is a good size. The result is a clear, nicely scaled image.

Power Mac vs. 68K vs. BackBurner

If you're doing 3D work, you really need to use a Power Mac. The PowerPC chip, which is the heart of the Power Mac, excels at floating-point calculations, and Infini-D is a heavily floating-point intensive application. Ray tracing, which is almost pure floating-point math, shows a 400 percent to 800 percent speed increase on a Power Mac versus an old 68K Macintosh. This isn't to say that Infini-D won't run on an older Macintosh—it will. Many Infini-D users still use 68K-based Macs, but your work will go a lot faster if you use a Power Mac.

If you're using Infini-D for high-resolution print work, or if you have several Macs sitting around your office displaying screen-saver art, you might want to consider BackBurner. *BackBurner* reads Infini-D files and distributes the work to multiple Macintoshes, making the whole process go faster. It can also suspend jobs, meaning you can interrupt a rendering and finish it later. You also can queue up multiple jobs on single or multiple Macintoshes to work over a weekend.

WORKING SMART

Try to beg, borrow, or steal a Power Mac. You'll see dramatic speed increases with Infini-D. If you do high-resolution work, need to interrupt jobs, queue multiple jobs, or have access to a network of Macs, consider BackBurner to lessen rendering time. There are BackBurner service centers that can help you do this.

QuickDraw 3D

QuickDraw 3D greatly speeds the process of scene setup and creation. However, the current version of QuickDraw 3D, as of the writing of this book, does not have final quality output capabilities. For this reason, the Specular renderers are recommended for final output, but Infini-D leaves the choice up to you. Infini-D supports QuickTime for rendering animation and scenes, and QuickDraw 3D for image files.

QuickDraw 3D uses Gouraud shading, but with some features that Specular's Gouraud doesn't support. For example, QuickDraw 3D does texture mapping in Gouraud, whereas Infini-D won't do texture mapping in less than Phong shading. On the other hand, using QuickDraw 3D, several Infini-D features are lost. Environment maps and procedural surfaces are not supported, and Infini-D's composed surfaces will not render in QuickDraw 3D.

With these feature losses and gains in mind, the most efficient use of QuickDraw 3D is as an interactive aid, showing models shaded during construction and setup. Also, use QuickDraw 3D for rendering images and animation when you need quick output. QuickDraw 3D produces fast, shaded animation previews to check motion and position. In a business situation, you might want to use QuickDraw 3D to produce for a client a demonstration of a work in progress. Then, when you are finished, use Specular's renderers for the final output. Remember the Universal Principle of 3D Computer Graphics— *The better it looks, the longer it takes.* Specular's renderers take longer, but the results are much nicer.

Output Tips: Working Well with Other Applications

Infini-D is only one step in the process of creating computer graphics and computer art. After the models are built, the scenes set up, and the animation animated, the job is only halfway finished. *Rendering* is the process of preparing your work for use in other applications. A still image, for example, might be opened in Photoshop to have effects applied, colors corrected, and then be printed. An animation might be rendered and brought into Adobe Premiere for editing, titling, and finally, outputting to video tape. These are all factors to consider when preparing final images and animation.

Resolution

For print work, resolution is the most important output decision. *Resolution* is the number of dots per inch, or *DPI*, in the rendered image. A standard computer screen usually has 72 dots, or pixels, for every inch of screen space. On-screen, images look crisp and clear at 72 DPI. Paper, however, requires a much higher resolution for clean image reproduction. Laser printers and inkjet printers typically can print at least 300 DPI.

Keep in mind that as resolution increases, rendering time increases exponentially. An image rendered at 300 DPI, for example, has four times as many pixels to calculate as a 150 DPI image, even though the resolution is only doubled. So, while print quality goes up with higher resolution, use the lowest resolution possible while still maintaining acceptable quality.

The final destination of your images ultimately determines the resolution. If the images are going to remain on a computer, the resolution can be left at Infini-D's default, 72 DPI. Thus, images intended for games, multimedia applications, World Wide Web pages, and so on can be rendered quickly at the low resolution of 72 DPI.

Animations, in most cases, also can be rendered at screen resolution. Television has lower resolution than the computer's screen, so, for outputting to video tape, 72 DPI is sufficient. Again, if the animation will be only on a computer screen, use 72 DPI. Film is the only exception. Film is very high resolution, and animation needs to be rendered accordingly. In this case, it is best to check the resolution and size of the particular film being used. All film is different.

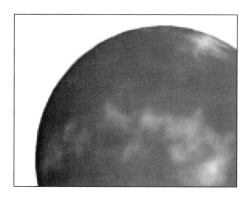

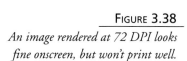

FIGURE 3.38

An image rendered at 72 DPI looks fine onscreen, but won't print well.

For print work, the resolution must be much higher. For color images, 300 DPI is normal, although some applications may require more. The quality of paper is important, as well as the number of colors, type of printing, and the smoothness desired. Check with the printer or publisher to see what resolution is needed for your situation.

When you have settled on a resolution, setting it in Infini-D is simple. Within the Render Image and Render Animation dialogs there is a pop-up menu. By default, the pop-up uses pixels as the units of measurement. Select the pop-up and choose inches. A resolution box will activate. Type the desired resolution. Infini-D calculates the image size based on the number of pixels per inch and the number of inches specified for the image's width and height.

QuickTime CODECs

A widely-known issue with computer graphics is the vast amount of disk space required for storage. Animations, in particular, can quickly use up large hard drives. To help with this problem, QuickTime provides *CODECs,* which are accessible from the Options button in the Save dialog. CODEC stands for COmpressor/DECompressor, and that is exactly what they do. CODECs are methods for compressing image data, so that less disk space is used, and decompressing image data quickly, so that it can be played back in real time.

Many add-on video capture/output boards, such as the Radius Video Vision package, include their own CODECs that must be used for optimal playback on that hardware. If you have extra hardware for video output, use that CODEC. If you are limited to Apple's built-in video output hardware, or if the animation will be only used on a computer and not printed to video, use one of QuickTime's six built-in CODECs: Animation, Cinepak, Component Video, Graphics, Photo-JPEG, and Video.

FIGURE **3.39**

300 DPI is ideal for print work.

QuickTime's Animation CODEC seems like the natural choice for Infini-D animation by name alone, and, in many cases, it is. Animation provides excellent image quality, is a relatively quick compressor (so it won't slow down rendering significantly), and plays back well on a reasonably fast computer. Of the six built-in compressors, Animation also provides the most options for bit-depth and is the only compressor that allows alpha channels. However, the Animation CODEC does not compress very effectively without losing image quality and can result in very large QuickTime movies. Animation uses what is called a *lossy compressor*—the more compression used, the lower the image quality. Using the 100% image quality setting provides almost no compression at all. Thus, the image quality is good, but the QuickTime movie is large. Image quality at 50% compresses the movie somewhat more, but the image quality is much poorer. If you have the space to store a large animation file, and need high quality, or if you're rendering with alpha channels, the Animation CODEC at 75% quality or higher is a good choice.

FIGURE 3.40

An image compressed with the Animation CODEC at the low-quality setting shows compression artifacts. A still image doesn't demonstrate the striping effect that Animation compression has, but in a video the striping is much more apparent.

FIGURE 3.41

The high-quality setting of the Animation CODEC eliminates a good deal of the compression artifacts, but produces much larger files.

Cinepak provides excellent compression and extremely smooth playback, but has much slower compression. Like Animation, Cinepak is a lossy compressor. Cinepak has much lower image quality than Animation, though, because of its higher compression ratio. Also, Cinepak is limited to grays, 256 colors, or millions of colors. Cinepak is a good choice if your disk space is limited or you need absolutely smooth playback and image quality is not critical.

The other four CODECs are not recommended for animation. Component Video does not let the user adjust the compression-to-quality ratio and is limited to color with no options for number of colors. Graphics also does not permit the user to adjust the compression ratio and is limited to 256 colors. Photo-JPEG can save in millions of colors but uses JPEG compression. JPEG has extremely lossy compression and decompresses somewhat slowly. Thus, image quality is poor and playback is not smooth. Video is another lossy compressor. With only a little compression, the Video image quality is still poor.

FIGURE 3.42

At the low-quality setting, Cinepak is extremely lossy and probably shouldn't be used except when disk space is extremely tight or the video must play back smoothly on a slow machine.

FIGURE 3.43

High-quality Cinepak compression has poorer image quality than Animation at low, but the file size is a fraction of an Animation compressed file.

There is a seventh option in the CODEC list. If compression is not necessary or it is important that no image quality be lost, select None. The images are saved as is, with no compression at all. If you plan to composite your animation with other video or animation in a video editing program, such as Adobe Premiere or Avid

Videoshop, no compression is a good choice. That way, rather than compressing and recompressing in each program, which results in very poor image quality, you can compress only the final, edited movie. This method, of course, requires more disk space.

FIGURE 3.44

Choosing no compression produces an image with no loss in image quality, which can then be composited with other animation and videos in post-production.

Using Alpha Channel Composition

An *alpha channel*, also known as a *mask*, is an outline or silhouette that saves the transparency and edge anti-aliasing information of a graphic. Stencils are a good metaphor for alpha channels. Take, for example, the large cardboard cut-out stencils used to paint words on roads. Imagine spray painting a piece of cardboard with the letter "E" cut out of it. The cardboard blocks the paint except where the letter "E" shows through. When you lift the cardboard, you'll have a perfectly painted "E" on the asphalt below.

Alpha channels work in similar ways, except in this case black pixels represent what is cut out and becomes the background (the cardboard), and white pixels represent what shows through, becoming the foreground (the paint). When an application like Photoshop uses alpha channels, it is almost always to mathematically blend two bitmaps together, usually in a simple composite. If you want to composite the letter "E" against a road background, any pixel that is black lets the road background show through, and any pixel that is white lets the letter "E" show through. Because alpha channels are 8-bit, meaning they have 256 levels of gray (at least good ones are), any pixel that is gray blends both the foreground and background together.

FIGURE **3.45**

Light shining through this object forms an "E" in the shadows on the ground, much the same way paint works with stencils and images work with alpha channels.

FIGURE **3.46**

The letter "E," the alpha channel rendered with it, and the final composition against a background.

The wonderful thing about Infini-D's alpha channels is that Infini-D does all of the work for you. If you create a 3D graphic of a cereal box, for example, Infini-D can create a pixel-perfect alpha channel, letting you composite that box onto a photograph of a store shelf. Better yet, Infini-D stores the anti-aliasing information for the box edges in the alpha channel, giving you a seamless digital composition with no edge whatsoever. (Warning: Some 3D programs actually output black and white alpha channels, meaning that the edges will be jaggy and harsh. If you are ever looking at a 3D program other than Infini-D, *make sure it outputs 8-bit alpha channels!* It is basically useless for digital composition if it does not.)

You can use Infini-D's alpha channels with other programs for either stills or animation. For example, you can export a 3D logo and composite it against a background in Photoshop. A common Infini-D/Photoshop technique for product visualizers is to render a 3D image of a packaging concept, and then composite it against a scanned photograph of a grocery shelf. This enables the client to see how the product concept looks with existing packaging. You also can use Infini-D with a digital video tool, such as Adobe Premiere or Avid Videoshop, to composite an animation of a 3D logo against moving video.

Infini-D Alpha Channels in PhotoShop: Radio Station Print Ad

Suppose you need to design a logo for a local radio station, WFCR. After creating the logo, an image needs to be placed in the background. Here's how it is done using Adobe PhotoShop.

1. **Open the file WFCR Rocks,** which is located on the CD-ROM included with this book. You can create any logo or image you want. We'll show you how to create this one in Chapter 7, "3D Text & Logos."

2. **Select "Window Options..." from the Windows menu.**

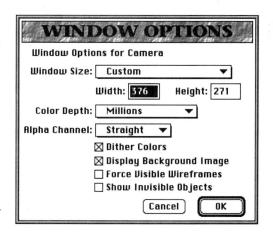

FIGURE 3.47

The Window Options dialog

3. **Select Millions in the Color Depth pop-up menu.**

4. **Select Straight in the Alpha Channel pop-up menu.**

5. **Click OK.**

6. **Render the logo with Best (Phong) shading and medium anti-aliasing.** The anti-aliasing information is stored in the alpha channel.

7. **Select "Save Image As..." from the File menu.** Save the image as a PICT file.

Alternatively, you can skip steps 2-7 and select Render Image... from the File menu. In the Render Image dialog, choose Millions of colors and a Straight alpha channel. Infini-D then renders the image and saves it to a file with the alpha channel information.

In Photoshop, open the rendered image and use the Load Selection command from the Select menu. This loads a selection based on the alpha channel that Infini-D has created. All you have to do is copy (⌘-C) and paste (⌘-V) to composite the image against any background. Photoshop uses Infini-D's anti-aliasing information to composite smoothly the logo against any background.

To enhance the natural 3D quality of Infini-D artwork, you also can use Photoshop to create a drop shadow based on the alpha channel. Flip through a PhotoShop effects book and apply any number of cool effects to the logo.

FIGURE 3.48
The rendered logo has an alpha channel defining the black background as transparent.

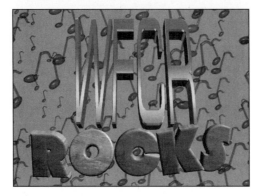

FIGURE 3.49
A background is seamlessly composited behind the logo.

FIGURE 3.50
A drop shadow is added to enhance the 3D effect.

Infini-D's Animated Alpha Channels in Adobe Premiere: Flying Logo

Infini-D is an ideal candidate for creating flying logos over scanned backgrounds or videos. Using QuickTime, an alpha channel can be stored with every frame of an animation, meaning that each frame can be seamlessly composited against a still or animated background.

For this example, we've created a logo for Cumulus Airlines and rendered a QuickTime movie with an alpha channel. Using the alpha channel,

the movie can be easily composited into Adobe Premiere.

Follow these steps to render an animation with an alpha channel.

1. **Open the Cumulus Airlines Infini-D file, found on the CD-ROM included with this book, or create your own flying logo.**

2. **Choose Render Animation from the File menu, or click the spool icon in the Sequencer.**

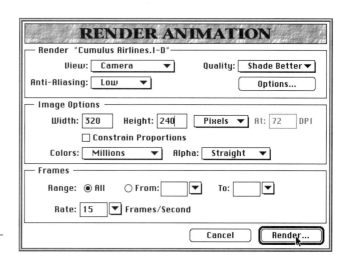

FIGURE 3.51

The Render Animation dialog

---

3. **Choose the view, quality, level of anti-aliasing, and frame size desired.**

4. **Choose Millions from the Colors pop-up menu and Straight from the Alpha pop-up menu.**

5. **Click Render.**

Make sure that QuickTime is selected in the Save As dialog box. Leave the QuickTime options alone for now. We'll talk about compression later. By default, Infini-D uses QuickTime options that support alpha channels.

To composite the logo, launch Adobe Premiere.

1. **Import the animation and whatever background you want.** The example file uses an image of clouds.

2. **Place the background in either Track A or Track B.** This is what you will composite against.

3. **Place the Infini-D QuickTime movie in the Super (S1) track.** The animation is superimposed on the background.

4. **With the Infini-D movie selected in the Super track, choose Transparency from the Clip menu.**

5. **Select Alpha Channel from the Transparency pop-up.**

FIGURE 3.52

The animation is rendered with an alpha channel ready for composition in Premiere.

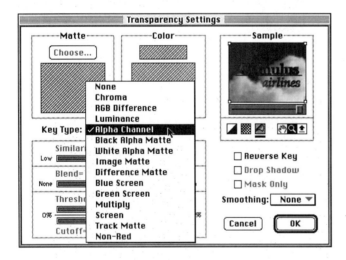

FIGURE 3.53

Premiere's Transparency dialog. Select Alpha Channel from the pop-up.

Premiere uses the alpha channel stored in every frame of the QuickTime movie to composite against the cloud background.

A couple of quick tips for using Infini-D movies in Premiere:

◆ Try changing the opacity of the alpha channel using the rubber band underneath the movie clip. This makes the logo fade in over the clouds as it approaches the camera.

◆ Try using the Image Pan filter to move or zoom the background. This can be a very powerful effect, especially when combined with 3D logos from Infini-D.

PhotoShop and Premiere are both very powerful programs. When your Infini-D images and animation have been imported into either program, there are limitless effects that you can apply to them. Don't stop at just compositing over background images or animation.

FIGURE 3.54

The logo animation blends seamlessly with the cloud background.

FIGURE 3.55

Adjusting opacity creates smooth fade ins and fade outs.

FIGURE 3.56

Adding an Image Pan to the cloud background makes the clouds move as the logo fades in.

Summary

This chapter has showed you how to use Infini-D to maximize your productivity and time. By this point, you should have a basic knowledge of Infini-D concepts and the Infini-D world in general. The next section will delve deeper into Infini-D and explain some concepts in detail.

Working with the Workshop

After the Infini-D basics are nailed down, in-depth exploration is necessary. With only the basics, you can begin experimenting and putting together some simple scenes, but with some knowledge of Infini-D's more powerful features, you can unlock many doors in your imagination. This chapter introduces the Infini-D Workshop and helps you build your own models to unlock those doors.

Workshop Basics

Infini-D 3.1 provides a powerful and extremely flexible Workshop for building all kinds of spline-based models. Spline curves enable you to create smooth surfaces without facets, and Infini-D's familiar tool set makes drawing simple. The flexibility of Infini-D's Workshop enables you to work in the configuration that best suits your work style. First, however, you must be familiar with the menus and windows of the Infini-D Workshop, as well as how models are built, at least on a conceptual level.

Introducing the Workshop

Infini-D's Workshop is composed of several elements. Up to five windows can be open to view and edit the model construction. There are three Path view windows, each of which can show any of six different Path views. The Cross section window displays each of the cross sections in a model, and the Object window displays the whole model in Wireframe or shaded with QuickDraw 3D.

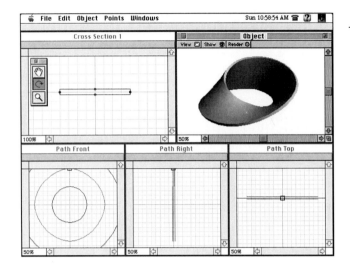

FIGURE **4.1**

Infini-D's Workshop displays up to five windows, and each shows a different view or a different part of a model.

Each of these windows has its own menu bar, with items that control settings specific to that window: path view, cross section, view angle, visible model elements, hidden model elements, and various grid and template settings. The windows can be set independently, so that you can

have two or three Path views with different settings showing different sides of the object.

The menu bar at the top of the screen controls global settings, or settings specific to the model being edited. These menus provide such controls as point type, mirroring method, and even special effects like twist and spiral.

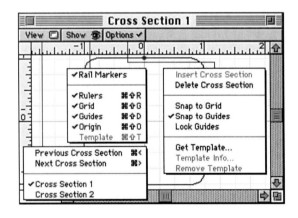

FIGURE **4.2**

The Cross Section view menus control the cross section that is viewed, the parts of the cross section that are visible, and provide snap-to and template controls.

FIGURE 4.3

The Path view menus determine the viewing angle and which Path view elements are visible. The Options menu is the same as the Cross Section view options menu, except that the controls are local to the active window.

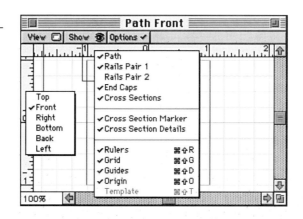

FIGURE 4.4

From the menus in the Object view, preset viewing angles are selected, perspective turned on and off, and various rendering options are adjusted.

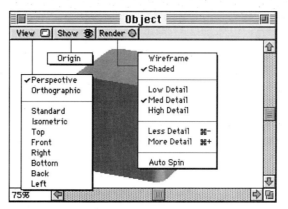

FIGURE 4.5

Menus on the main menu bar control global, object-specific, and point- or path-specific attributes. The Object menu shown here includes some special effects, such as Bevel, Spiral, and Twist.

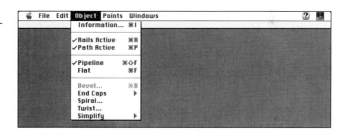

The Workshop is controlled via a context-sensitive Toolbox. The Toolbox displays the set of tools available to the current window. By selecting the Cross section window, for example, the Toolbox displays a full set of drawing tools. Selecting a Path view shrinks the Toolbox slightly, because some tools available for drawing cross sections are not appropriate for the Path views. Lastly, selecting the Object view shrinks the Toolbox considerably to only the Hand, Rotate, and Zoom tools, because the Object view is only for viewing the model.

Finally, at the top of the screen, just below the main menu bar, is the Info bar. The Info bar displays information, such as mouse location, rotation angle, and position changes. Information is displayed as it occurs. That is, the rotation information only appears while something is being rotated, and position changes are only reported when something is being moved.

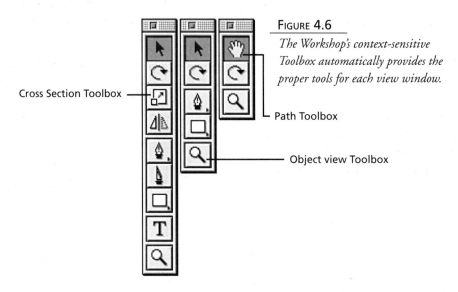

Cross Section Toolbox

FIGURE 4.6

The Workshop's context-sensitive Toolbox automatically provides the proper tools for each view window.

Path Toolbox

Object view Toolbox

🍎 **File Edit Object Points Windows**

x:0.5"   y:0.3"   r:60.6°   ∆:0.6"

FIGURE 4.7

Located immediately below the menu bar, the Info bar displays current data. For example, this Info bar is displaying the current X and Y coordinates of the mouse, along with the angle of the current rotation and the change in position.

Model Construction

Infini-D uses a *path-profile* method for building objects; each object is defined by a path and a set of profiles, or cross sections. Also, there are a two pairs of *rails* that define the outside of an object. Using these three elements, many complex objects can be modeled easily.

The path acts as a sort of spine for an object. It runs straight through the center of the object and can be used to bend the object or define curves. Figure 4.8 shows a wine glass. The path is the line running up the center. By selecting and rotating parts of the path, the wine glass can be bent.

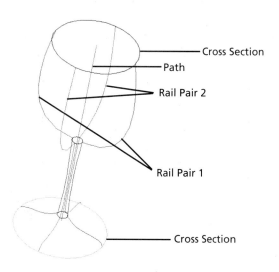

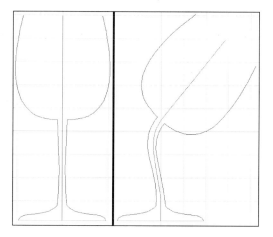

Along the path are cross sections. These act as ribs along the spine and define the shape of an object. For example, a circular cross section creates a round object like the wine glass. A square cross section gives the object four corners. A star-shaped cross section makes the object star-shaped. You can have as many cross sections as you want. Figures 4.10–4.13 show some examples of how cross sections affect the shape of an object.

Last, the two pairs of rails define the scale of the cross sections. That is, you don't need to build a separate cross section just to taper the sides of an object. The wine glass in figure 4.8 requires only one cross section because the shape is defined by the rails. The glass is round from top to bottom. The single starting cross section defines the shape, while the rails scale that shape and define a base, stem, and finally the glass itself. By editing just the rails, the glass shape can be changed to make different types of glasses, or make the glass do things a real glass would have trouble doing. Figures 4.14–4.17 demonstrate how the rails control the object's shape.

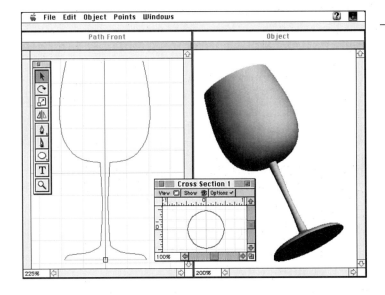

FIGURE **4.10**

A normal wine glass is created using a circular cross section.

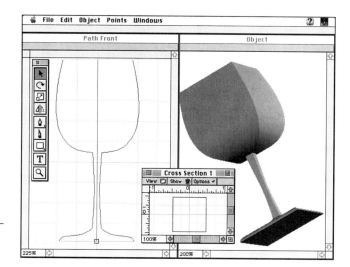

FIGURE 4.11

By changing the cross section to square, the glass becomes square.

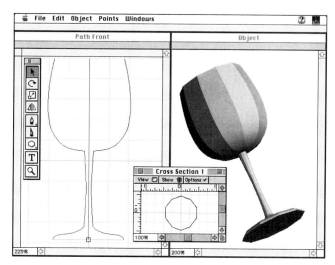

FIGURE 4.12

A ten-sided cross section gives the glass a faceted look.

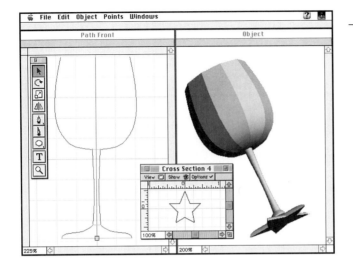

FIGURE **4.13**

Using multiple cross sections, the glass changes shape. In this example, the base is star shaped, the stem is round, and the glass is faceted.

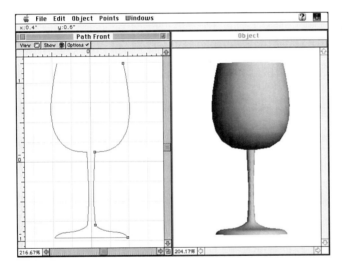

FIGURE **4.14**

A normal wine glass is made by drawing wine glass–shaped rails.

FIGURE **4.15**

Dragging the rails down and away from the center squashes and stretches the glass.

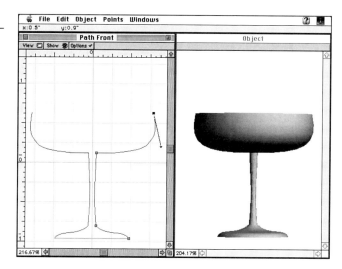

FIGURE **4.16**

The rails can be curved up and around to create different shapes.

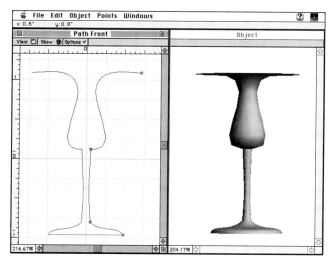

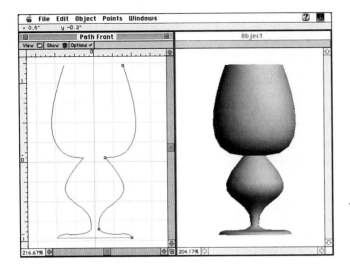

FIGURE 4.17

All parts of a rail can be edited. Here the stem of the glass bulges when the rails defining the stem are pulled out.

Object Lesson: Building a Wine Glass

As an exercise in building models in Infini-D, here's how to construct a wine glass. Infini-D has a wine glass as a default lathe object, and this tutorial shows you how it is built.

1. **Select and place a lathe object in the World.** Any object can be placed, but by using a lathe object, Infini-D automatically configures the Workshop for building lathe objects, such as the wine glass.

2. **Enter the Workshop by double-clicking the lathe object.** You also can get into the Workshop by selecting the object and choosing Edit Model from the Model menu. Infini-D opens the Workshop and arranges the windows.

3. **With the Pen tool, define the side of the wine glass in the Path view.** The Pen tool functions much like the Pen tools of Adobe Illustrator and Adobe Photoshop. Click to define a point and drag handles to adjust the curve. The point type can be changed in the Points menu. Because the Workshop is set up to draw lathe objects, rails will be active. Draw with the Pen tool while no points are selected to draw a new rail.

FIGURE **4.18**

A wine glass built using the lathe layout of Infini-D's Workshop.

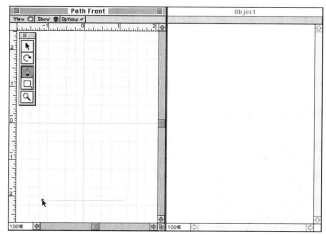

FIGURE **4.19**

Place a single point with the Pen tool. Infini-D automatically puts a cross section at that first point.

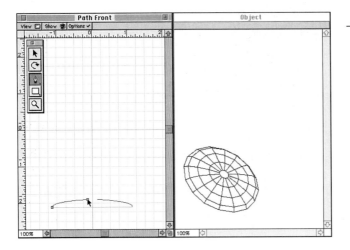

FIGURE 4.20

Place a second point to create the base of the glass. This time click and drag to place the point so the path between the points is curved.

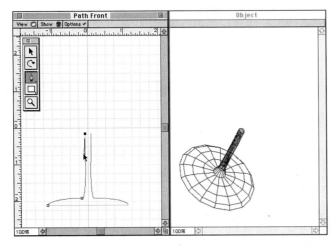

FIGURE 4.21

A third point defines the stem of the glass.

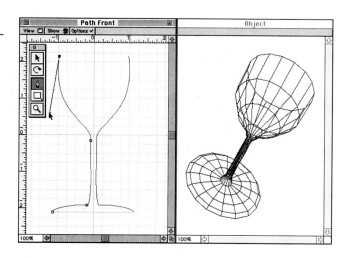

FIGURE 4.22

The fourth and final point creates the top of the glass.

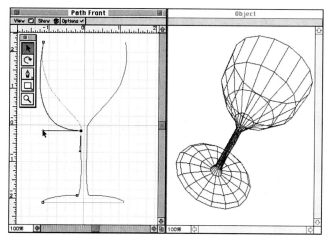

FIGURE 4.23

After all points are placed, adjustments are made to the point handles.

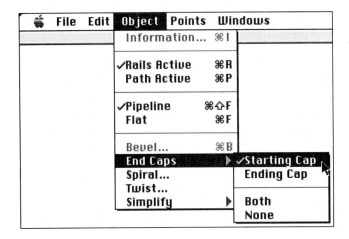

FIGURE 4.24

Finally, the End Caps are set to Starting Cap only. This leaves the top of the glass open, but caps the bottom.

Infini-D automatically fills in the details. The first point is the cross section for the model, and, because the default cross section for a lathe object is a circle, the glass will be round. Lathe objects also have Mirror 4-ways turned on by default, so that Infini-D uses the single rail you draw to define all four rails.

After you have drawn the wine glass, there are many things you can do with it. The shape, for example, can be changed by opening the Cross section window and replacing the circle with another shape. Delete the circle and draw a square to create a square wine glass. You also can add cross sections to change the shape at certain points. Make the path active and the cross section marker visible. Drag the marker (a small square on the path) along the path to the point where you want the shape to change. Select Insert Cross section from the Options menu in the Path window. Open the Cross section view and change the new cross section.

Object Types

There are several different types of objects referred to in this book, and you should know what those are. This does not mean, however, that Infini-D is limited to building only the object types listed. For the most part, the object type is unimportant, because Infini-D has only one modeler for building all object types.

Infini-D has three main object types: *lathe, extrude,* and *freeform.* A lathe object is an object built as if it were made on a real lathe. That is, a single silhouette-like outline of the object is spun around a vertical axis (see Figure 4.25). Infini-D's rails provide the outlines to be lathed in this case.

Extrude objects are a little simpler. An extruded object is just an outline that is given depth. Text objects, for example, are created by giving depth to an outline of the text. Infini-D uses the cross section as the outline to extrude.

Freeform objects are not limited like lathe and extrude objects. Freeform objects are defined by a freely adjustable combination of cross sections, rails, and a path.

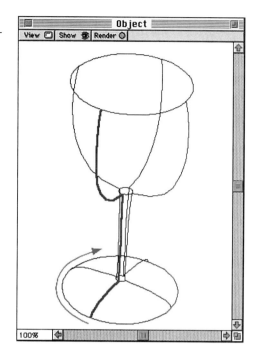

FIGURE 4.25

A lathe object is a single rail, the bold line, that is revolved around a vertical axis to create an object. The path of revolution is indicated here by the arrow.

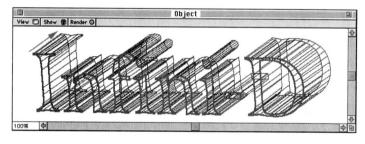

FIGURE 4.26

Extrude objects give depth to a cross section. The arrow indicates the path of extrusion.

There are many other object types that fall into subclasses of the three main types. A *partial lathe*, for example, is just a lathe object whose cross section has been cut, so that it is not a complete circle. A *path extrusion object* is an extrude object whose path has been bent. *Lofted objects* have cross sections with different shapes. Many other object types are possible, but with Infini-D's Workshop you don't need to concern yourself with the type of object. Just build the model in whichever Workshop layout works best.

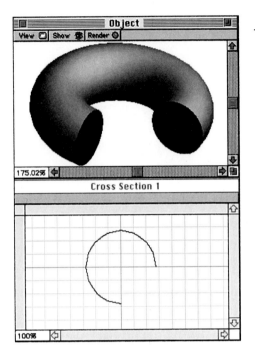

FIGURE 4.27

A partial lathe is made by cutting sections out of the cross section.

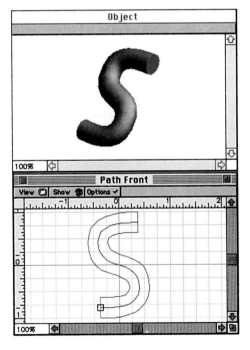

FIGURE 4.28

Path extrusion objects are extrusion objects whose paths have been modified.

FIGURE 4.29

A lofted object has two or more cross sections with different shapes.

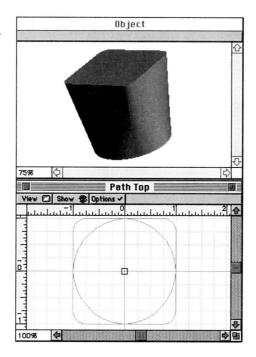

Workshop Layouts

Infini-D uses a *single-modeler* approach to building objects. That is, there is one Workshop where all types of objects are built, whether they are lathe objects, extrude objects, lofted objects, or any other type of objects. This is accomplished by providing user-configurable *layouts.*

Layouts are saved sets of window placements, sizes, and settings. By rearranging the windows, showing and hiding different parts of the model in each window, and changing some object-based settings the type of object built can be completely changed. For example, the lathe layout displays the Path Front window with rails enabled, mirrored four ways, and the path disabled. The cross section for a lathe is predefined as a circle. Thus, by drawing a single, new rail, you can build lathe objects. The extrude layout, on the other hand, only displays the Cross section window. Because extrude objects have a straight path and rails, there is no need to have the Path views active.

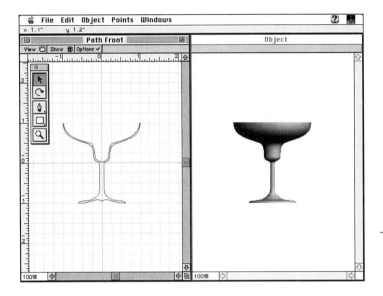

FIGURE **4.30**

The lathe layout is set up with a larger Path view window for drawing rails.

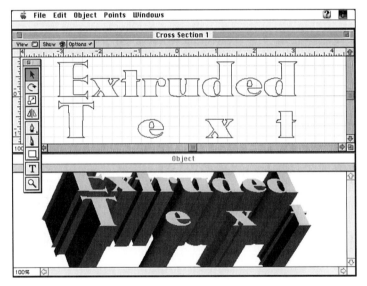

FIGURE **4.31**

The extrusion layout provides a large Cross Section window, oriented specifically for creating text.

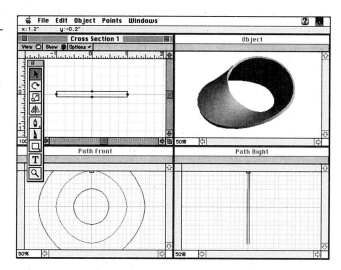

FIGURE 4.32

Freeform objects are best modeled with multiple views, which the freeform layout displays.

Infini-D provides six useful layouts: two lathe layouts, two extrusion layouts, and two freeform layouts. While these might be enough to work with, you might find yourself frequently rearranging the windows, showing and hiding rails and paths, and changing mirroring modes or any number of other settings. In such cases, Infini-D enables you to save layouts. In the Windows menu, at the top of the Layout submenu, there is a Save option. Follow these steps to take advantage of this feature.

1. **Set up the windows exactly as you want them and make sure all window and object settings are adjusted correctly.** You cannot edit a saved layout except by removing and resaving it, so it is best to set it up correctly the first time.

2. **Select Save from the Layout submenu in the Windows menu.**

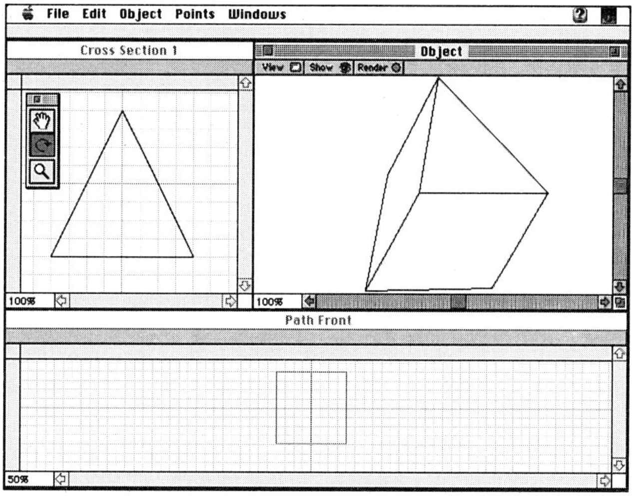

FIGURE 4.33

An alternate path extrusion layout is shown here, ready to be saved.

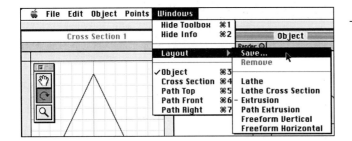

FIGURE **4.34**

Select Save from the layout pop-up under the Windows menu.

3. **Enter an appropriate name for the layout.** Because Infini-D permits you to give different layouts the same name, use names that are suggestive of what the layout looks like so as not to lose track of which layout is which.

4. **Click OK.** Infini-D saves the new layout at the bottom of the Layout menu. Now, whenever you want to use your layout, just select its name from the Layout submenu.

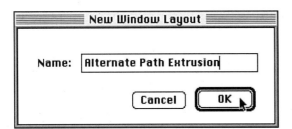

FIGURE **4.35**

"Alternate Path Extrusion" indicates the type of layout being saved.

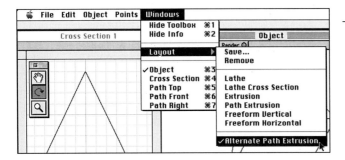

FIGURE **4.36**

Saved layouts can be recalled by selecting them from the bottom of the Layout submenu.

Infini-D saves layouts in the Workshop Prefs file found in the Specular folder in the System's Preferences folder. If you ever switch machines or reinstall your System for any reason, you might want to copy your Workshop Prefs first. That way, you can move the Prefs file back into the Specular folder after the machine switch or system reinstall, and the layouts should reappear in the Infini-D Workshop.

Tricks with Tools

After you've gotten the hang of Workshop control and model construction, take a look at the Toolbox. Remember, the Workshop Toolbox is context-sensitive, so it will be different depending on the active window. For the sake of clarity,

I'll refer to the three modes of the Workshop Toolbox as three separate toolboxes.

The Workshop tools are designed to be as familiar as the World tools are. The Cross section view toolbox has Rotate, Scale, and Flip tools, along with a Pen, Pencil, and even a Razor tool for slicing cross section outlines. All of these tools are modeled after tools in other popular drawing packages, so if you are familiar with Adobe Illustrator or Adobe Photoshop, you should have some idea how to use them already. Incidentally, the Cross section view toolbox contains all but one of the available Workshop tools; the other two toolboxes are subsets of the Cross section view tools. The exception is the Object view toolbox, which has a Hand tool.

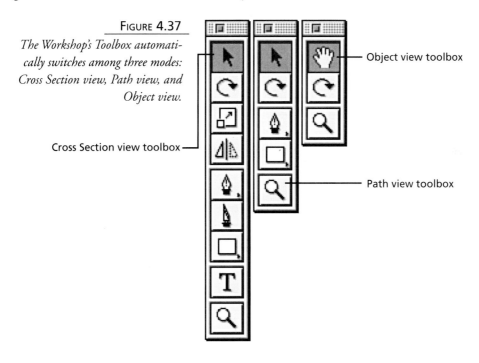

FIGURE 4.37

The Workshop's Toolbox automatically switches among three modes: Cross Section view, Path view, and Object view.

Object view toolbox

Cross Section view toolbox

Path view toolbox

The Rotate Tool

The Rotate tool is available in all the toolbox modes, although it works somewhat differently depending on the mode. In the Cross section view toolbox, the Rotate tool can rotate any number of points around any center of rotation. To rotate points, select those you want to rotate using the normal arrow cursor. Then, use the Rotate tool to drag the points in a circle around the centerpoint. By default, the center of rotation is the center of the grid. That point can be moved by a single click with the Rotate tool. Just click where you want the center to be and a small cross hair will appear where the new center is.

TIP

Any combination of points in a cross section can be selected for rotation. Thus, you can select an entire cross section using Select All („-A) and spin the whole outline (Figure 4.38), or you can select a small number of points and rotate sections of an outline (Figure 4.39). Also, the selected points do not need to be contiguous. You can select points that are not next to each other and rotate. Points in between will not be affected by the rotation (Figure 4.40).

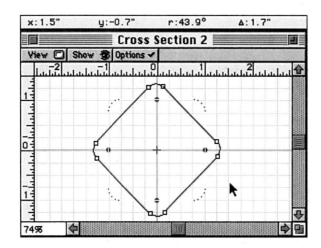

FIGURE **4.38**

A whole cross section is rotated by selecting the outline and dragging with the Rotate tool.

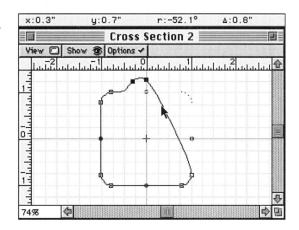

FIGURE 4.39

Selecting specific parts of a cross section will rotate only those peices.

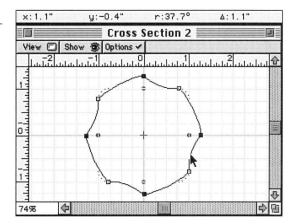

FIGURE 4.40

Selected parts need not be contiguous. Every other point is rotated in this example.

The Rotate tool works in basically the same way in the Path views. In the Path views you can select any combination of rail points and path points, and the center of rotation is defined by a single click.

Object Lesson: Creating a Bend

Objects can be bent very effectively using the Rotate tool in the Path views. Here's how:

1. **Make the path and rails active.** The rails need to be active so that the shape they define is not affected. If rails are inactive, rotation will reset them to flat, albeit bent rails. The path must be active. Because it is the spine of the object, it needs to stay in the center of the object.

2. **Select the points between which the bend will be made.**

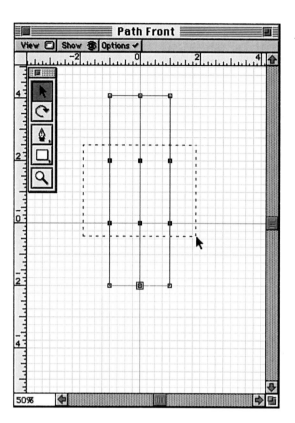

FIGURE 4.41

Use the marquee to drag-select the points around the bend.

3. **Change the selected points' type to curved.** In order to make the bend smooth, the path and rails need to curve. If the points are plain, the path and rails will remain straight lines, creating faceted, polygonal bends.

4. **Select the points to be rotated on both the path and the rails.** You want Infini-D to rotate a section of the object as if it were solid, so you need to select all the points you want to rotate.

5. **Define a centerpoint at the base of the rotation section.** To create a bend, the object is turned at the intersection of the rotated section and the unrotated section. The path point at that intersection is a good place to put the rotation centerpoint. In this case, place the centerpoint in the middle of the segment to be bent, as shown in Figure 4.44.

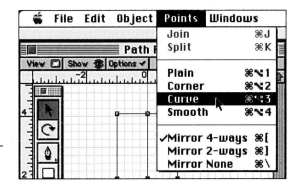

FIGURE **4.42**

Change the point type from the Points menu to create curved points.

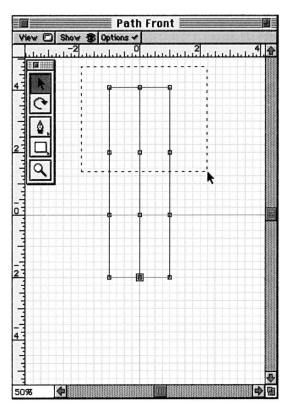

FIGURE **4.43**

Using the marquee, select the points to be rotated.

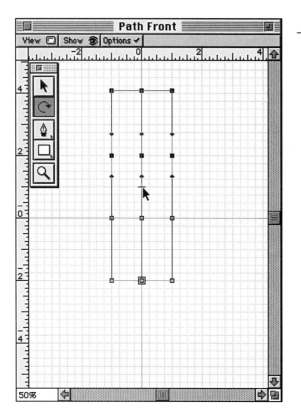

FIGURE **4.44**

Move the center of rotation by clicking once with the Rotate tool.

6. **Click and drag to rotate the selected points.** Be careful not to rotate too far. Although it's easy to bend objects farther than would be physically possible in the real world, Infini-D still has some trouble making impossible bends look good. If you bend too far, the object will begin to pinch and fold over itself.

TIP

Bending incrementally creates smoother curves. Sometimes Infini-D has trouble making large rotations all at once. To create smoother bends, try rotating a little, releasing the mouse, and then rotating again. For example, to make a 90% turn, you might rotate 30% and stop. Then rotate another 30% and stop. Repeat once more and the rotation is complete. By doing the rotations a little at a time, Infini-D can build better curves and the resulting object will be smoother. Note that this is not always necessary. Usually, Infini-D can build smooth curves anyway. Try this method if your curves aren't as smooth as you'd like.

FIGURE 4.45

Click and drag with the Rotate tool to rotate the selected points around the defined center of rotation.

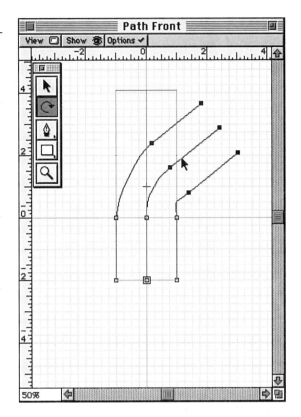

FIGURE 4.46

The newly bent tube is drawn in the Object view.

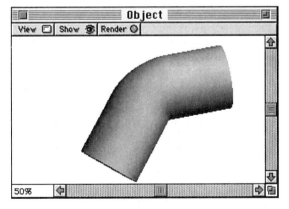

TIP

Use several separate rotation points to create longer bends. Remember that the Rotate tool is not specifically a bending tool. Rotating a section only spins those points around the defined rotational centerpoint.

As a result, the segments of rail and path bend immediately at the rotation point. The rest of the selected points only spin; the rails and path remain straight. If you want to create a bend that spans more than two path points, you have to use more than one rotation. Perform the first rotation, deselect both path and rail points at the rotation point, and perform the second rotation. Don't forget to move the centerpoint to the new bend point.

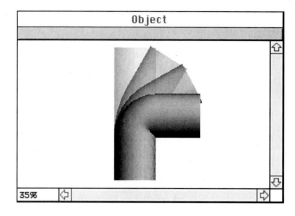

FIGURE 4.47

By bending in increments, Infini-D can sometimes create smoother curves.

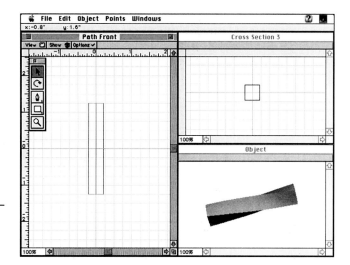

FIGURE 4.48

This twisted object is made with three cross sections. A normal bend cannot be applied to the whole object.

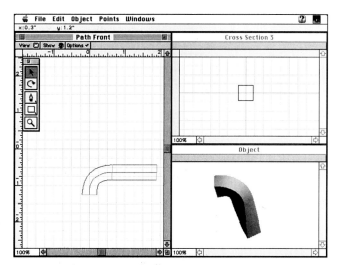

FIGURE 4.49

The first section is bent halfway to create part of the whole bend.

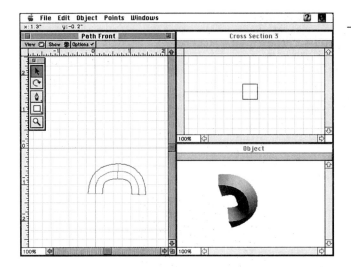

FIGURE **4.50**

A second bend on the second section completes the curve.

The Scale Tool

Typically, a Scale tool is thought of as something that changes the size of an outline. Not so with the Scale tool, third from the top in the Cross section Toolbox, in Infini-D's Workshop. By selecting all points on a cross section, that cross section can be scaled up and down (holding Shift will constrain the scaling), but, like the Rotate tool, any number and combination of points can be selected for scaling. This capability enables more flexibility than a standard scale-all tool. The centerpoint can be moved as well, with a single click from the Rotate tool. Moving the centerpoint enables outlines to be scaled in specific directions. Figures 4.51–4.55 show some examples of the Scale tool in use.

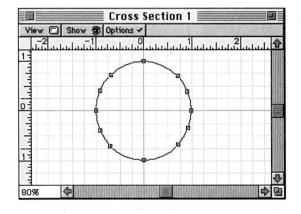

FIGURE **4.51**

Start with a normal circular cross section and add eight extra points.

FIGURE 4.52

This shape is created by selecting the three center points on either side and scaling.

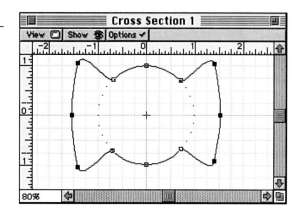

FIGURE 4.53

To make a star-like shape, select every other point and scale.

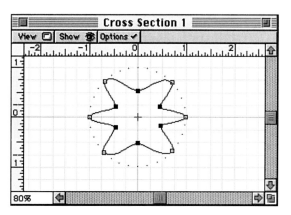

FIGURE 4.54

Select the three top points, three bottom points, and one point from either side to scale into an arrow.

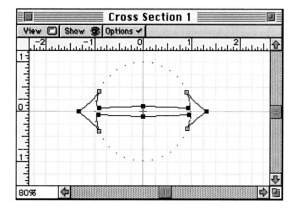

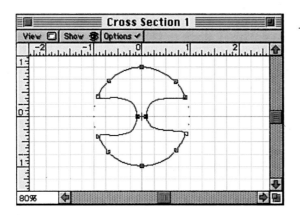

FIGURE **4.55**

The two side points are scaled into the center to make this shape.

The Flip Tool

The Flip tool, fourth from the top in the Cross section Toolbox, is a little trickier than the first two, although just as useful. When the Flip tool is selected, a small crosshair appears at the center of the window, just like the centerpoint-marking crosshairs of the Rotate and Scale tools. This one, however, does not define a centerpoint. Instead, this crosshair marks one end of a line. The other end of the line is defined by whatever point you click to begin the flip. Like the other tools, flips can be performed on all or part of a cross section. So, to flip a cross section, select the outline or points to flip, click once to set the crosshair at one end of the flip axis, and click and hold to set the other end. While still holding the mouse button, drag very slightly. The cross section will flip over the invisible line between the mouse cursor and the crosshairs. *But be careful.* After the selected points have flipped, they will begin to rotate around a centerpoint exactly midway between the mouse and the crosshair. If you don't want any rotation, a tiny nudge is all Infini-D needs to flip.

Use the Flip tool as a mirror.

Infini-D doesn't provide any mirroring functionality in the Cross section views.

To create symmetrical cross sections, follow these steps.

1. **Draw one half of the cross section.** Make this one perfect because any adjustments made later will not be updated automatically. You can leave the ends of the outline open because the outline can be closed when the other half is drawn.

2. Select the half cross section by clicking the outline.

3. **Copy and paste the outline.** Infini-D's Workshop has no Duplicate command, but by copying and pasting from the Edit menu, you get a duplicate copy of the outline.

4. **Flip one copy of the outline using the Scale tool.** Define the mirroring axis along the edge of the object you want to mirror. For example, if the outline was drawn on the left side of the screen and needs to be mirrored onto the right side, click once at the top of the cross section window in the center. Then, click the bottom center of the window and drag slightly. The outline will be mirrored onto the right side of the screen.

FIGURE 4.56

The dotted line between the cursor and the crosshair is the invisible axis Infini-D uses to flip an outline.

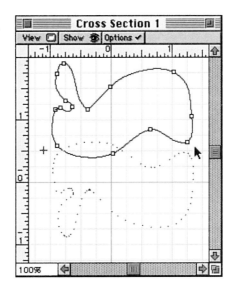

FIGURE 4.57

One half of the cross section is drawn, ready to be mirrored.

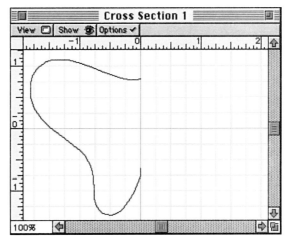

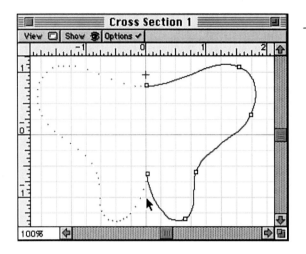

FIGURE 4.58

Define an axis and flip a copy of the outline to create a mirror image of the original.

5. **Select a pair of end points of the two halves.** The two ends must be joined separately, so that Infini-D knows which points are meant to be joined. Repeat steps 5 and 6 for each end of the outline halves.

6. **Choose Join (⌘-J) from the Points menu.** The ends of the two halves are

joined into a single, solid outline. If the end points of the two halves are far apart, they are joined into single points. If the end points are too far apart, Infini-D draws lines between the end points to join them. It's a good idea to position the two halves before joining to avoid having to clean up Infini-D's joints afterward.

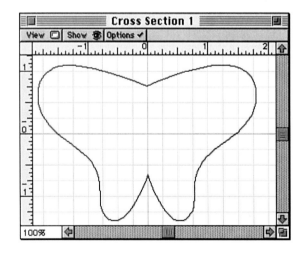

FIGURE 4.59

Two halves of a cross section are joined into single points.

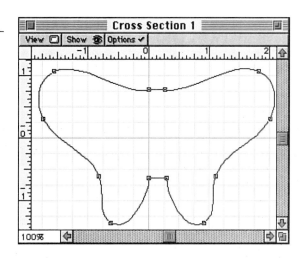

FIGURE **4.60**

If the two halves are farther apart when joined, Infini-D draws a line between the end points.

The Pen and Pencil Tools

Path views and the Cross section view have two tools for drawing: the Pen and the Pencil. The Pen works like Illustrator's and Photoshop's Pen tools and the Pencil is a freehand drawing tool. Both tools create fully editable, spline outlines.

Using the Pen tool is as simple as pointing and clicking. Point to the area where the line should start and click. A single point is placed. Move to another area and click again. A second point is placed with a line between the two. Click again elsewhere and a third point is created with another joining line. Continue pointing and clicking until the outline is finished. You may notice,

however, that this creates straight lines. With a Spline Pen tool, curves are possible.

To create curving lines, hold down the mouse button when you click to create a point. Drag away from the newly placed point. Handles sprout from the point, and the newly created line begins to curve. Move the handle around to see how the curve responds. The farther the handle is dragged, the more extreme the curve. Rotate the handle around the point to adjust the angle of the curve. Release the handle when you have adjusted the curve to your satisfaction. Don't worry if you don't like the curve when you release the handle. You can always use the Arrow tool to adjust handles and move points.

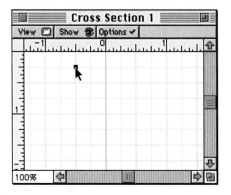

FIGURE **4.61**

A single click with the Pen creates a single point.

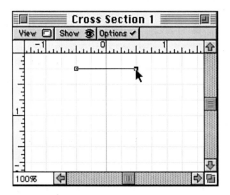

FIGURE **4.62**

A second click elsewhere makes a second point, and a line is drawn between the two.

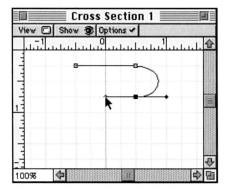

FIGURE **4.63**

A click and drag with the Pen tool to pull handles out of a new point. These handles control the curve of the connecting line.

The Pencil tool is even simpler than the Pen tool. To use the Pencil, simply click and drag. Like a standard pencil in a drawing or paint program, a line appears along the path you trace with the mouse. The difference, however, is that Infini-D's Pencil draws a spline outline that can be edited via points and handles, just like a Pen tool outline. Use the Arrow tool to edit pencil-drawn outlines.

TIP

Hold ⌘ and click a line segment to make curve adjustments. A hidden function of Infini-D's spline curves is temporarily enabled. While holding the ⌘ key down, click and drag a curve between two points. The curve itself grows or shrinks, depending on the direction it is dragged. Infini-D is actually dragging the handles of both points at each end of the curve. The angle of the handles won't change; Infini-D just drags them in and out, so that the curve only gets more or less extreme. It's a quick way to make slight adjustments to the tightness of a curve.

The Razor Tool

Outlines often need to be split apart or broken. There is a command that splits a point into two separate points, but sometimes outlines need to be broken at an arbitrary spot along a curve. Enter Infini-D's Razor tool. One click and drag with the Razor tool defines a *slice*. The outline is split apart wherever the slice crosses it. Drag the Razor tool across a circle, and the path is split into two semicircles. The Razor tool is of particular use in conjunction with the Join tool. Two overlapping polygons can be joined by slicing them open, deleting the overlapping parts, and joining the open ends (Figures 4.68 and 4.69).

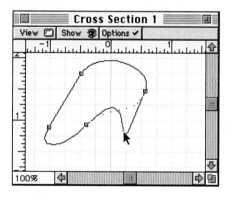

FIGURE 4.64

Holding the ⌘ key while clicking the curve between two points enables you to drag the curve itself, instead of adjusting the handles manually.

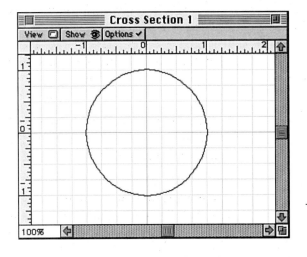

FIGURE 4.65
A cross section can be cut open anywhere using the Razor tool.

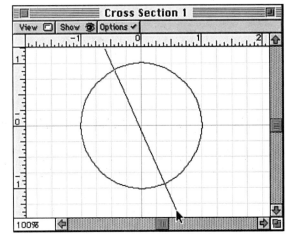

FIGURE 4.66
Click and drag the Razor across the cross section to cut the outline.

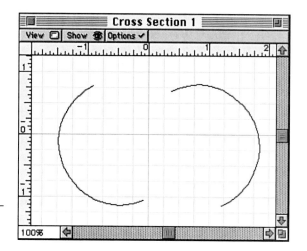

FIGURE 4.67

The outline is cut where the Razor tool crosses it.

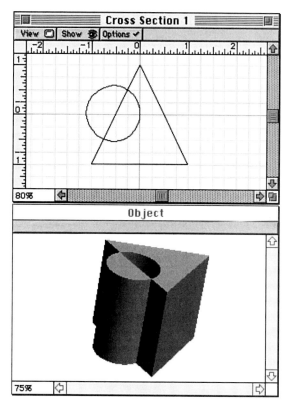

FIGURE 4.68

Two overlapping outlines normally cut holes through an object where the overlap occurs.

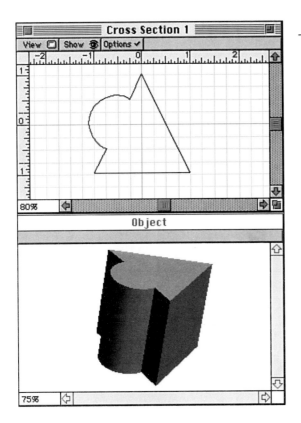

FIGURE **4.69**

Using the Razor tool, the overlap can be cut out and the outlines joined to create a single outline.

The Polygon Tools

Infini-D's Workshop provides a set of four polygon drawing tools for creating cross sections, paths, and rails. These are useful for creating shapes that are difficult to draw by hand. It's hard for example, to draw a perfect circle even using the Pen tool. The four tools are a Rectangle, Ellipse, Rounded Rectangle, and a Hexagon. Infini-D helps out even further by following standard Macintosh key modifiers. In this case, holding the Shift key while placing a polygon constrains the polygon to a 1-to-1 aspect ratio (all sides are the same length; a square instead of a rectangle, for example). Also, holding the ⌘ key causes Infini-D to draw the polygon with its center exactly at (0,0) on the grid.

When drawing in the Cross section view, the Polygon tools behave like regular drawing tools. In the Path views, they draw somewhat differently. In the Path views, you must pay attention to what model parts are active. If the rails are active, the Polygon tools will replace the rails, even if the path is also active. If the rails are disabled and the path is active, the Polygon tools will replace the path. Thus, by enabling the rails, it is possible to make rails that loop (Figure 4.70). By disabling the rails and enabling the path, the path can be made to wrap around and connect to itself (Figure 4.71).

FIGURE **4.70**

With rails enabled, the Polygon tools draw looping rails.

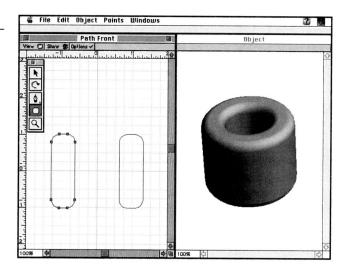

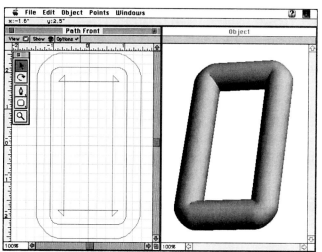

It might seem odd that one of the four basic Polygon tools is a hexagon. It turns out that the hexagon is actually a user-definable generic Polygon tool. Double-clicking the Polygon tools in the Toolbox opens the Shape Preferences dialog. The number of sides of the generic Polygon tool can be changed, as well as the radius of rounded rectangle corners.

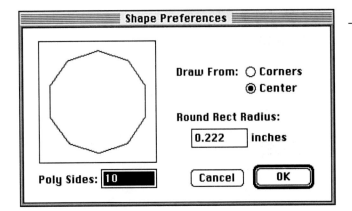

FIGURE 4.72

The Shape Preferences dialog contains the number of polygon sides setting and the Rounded Rect Corner Radius setting.

The Workshop Text Tool

While text can be placed in the World without entering the Workshop at all, World text is limited to the fonts installed in the system. Workshop text, however, can be edited in any way.

Text placed with the Workshop Text tool is drawn as spline outlines, so that it is completely editable and can be distorted, flipped, rotated, and rearranged on a letter-by-letter and point-by-point basis.

FIGURE 4.73

Regular text created in the Workshop is initially identical to World text. There are some small imperfections where the characters overlap.

FIGURE **4.74**

Because this text was created in the Workshop, the overlap can be removed using the Razor tool and the Join command.

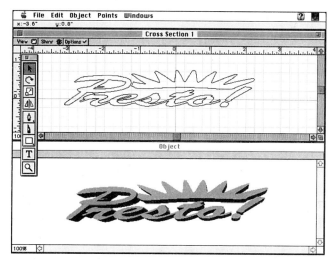

FIGURE **4.75**

Text can be scaled, rearranged, and more shapes can be added.

The Zoom Tool

All three toolbox modes share the Zoom tool. It functions in exactly the same way as the World Zoom tool: click or click and drag a rectangle to zoom in, Option-click to zoom out. Also, note that by double-clicking the Zoom tool in the toolbox, you can re-center windows and zoom them to 100%. It's like a reset button for the active window.

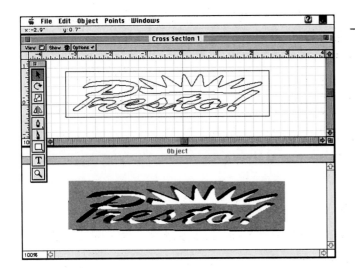

FIGURE **4.76**

Text created in the Workshop can even be punched out of another object by surrounding the text with another shape.

Working in 3D Space with 2D Tools

One of the most difficult aspects of 3D modeling and animation is the transition from two dimensions into three. The computer screen is a two-dimensional space. It has no depth. The mouse is also restricted to two dimensions. Lifting the standard mouse does not move the cursor into or out of the screen. Yet, despite this, the point is to create 3D spaces and 3D objects. How, then, can a two-dimensional pointing device control a two-dimensional image of a three-dimensional space?

Infini-D's approach to this problem is unique. Instead of attempting to represent three-dimensional space in 2D, Infini-D provides many different, two-dimensional ways to view a scene. Like a Computer Aided Design (CAD) program, Infini-D has six different orthogonal (no perspective) windows that enable the user to see all sides of a scene. The tools generally work in two dimensions as well. The exception is the virtual trackball. It is a representation of three-dimensional movement.

The Infini-D Workshop takes the same approach. All drawing views are two-dimensional, as are the tools used within them. Like the World views, Workshop Path views can look at an object from six sides. This means that the user must interpret the two-dimensional views in 3D. While this is not a difficult thing (we do it all the time when watching TV, movies, and computer screens), it can take some getting used to. Of course, Infini-D always provides a 3D view of objects and spaces; the World has camera views and the Workshop has the Object view. Still, it is up to the user to visualize how the two-dimensional views relate to the three-dimensional views. Here are a few tips to help the visualization process.

◆ **Switch views often.** The best way to see how things fit together is to look at them from different views. In the Path views, use the View menu liberally. You might have to switch rail pairs on or off, depending on the view. By looking at different sides of the object, you can see how the parts correspond to each other and where they fit into the three-dimensional Object view.

◆ **Match the Object view with the Path views.** The Object view has the same View menu as the Path views. By selecting the same view for both the Path views and the Object view, you can see a wireframe or shaded representation of the paths you are building. Then, use the Rotate tool to turn the Object view very slightly. By turning the view just a little, other sides' intersections with the current view become apparent.

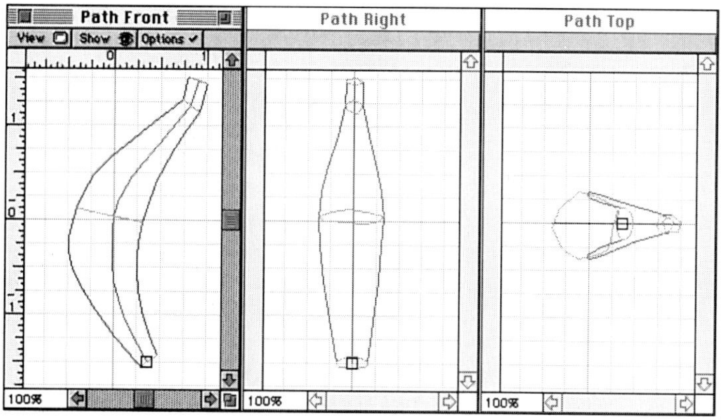

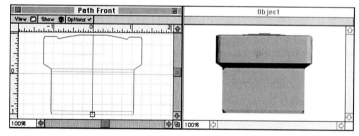

FIGURE 4.77

Multiple Path views show objects from all angles. Three windows are open, but any window can show any Path view by selecting another from the View menu.

FIGURE 4.78

Aligning the Path views with the Object views helps by displaying a shaded or wireframe representation of exactly what the rails are defining.

- **Take advantage of the virtual trackball in the Object view.** The virtual trackball rotation tool in the Object view enables rotation. Spin it to see odd angles and view the object from positions not available in the standard views. With QuickDraw 3D, there is even an Autospin feature. With Autospin, QuickDraw 3D automatically keeps the object rotating at the speed and in the direction specified by the initial spin. Autospinning lets you work in other windows while providing many different viewing angles of your objects.

Object Lesson: Creating a Tube Chair

The best way to learn Infini-D's Workshop is, of course, practice. Some simple lathe or extrude objects help, but an object whose shape isn't defined by a single view is even better. The tube chair is a perfect example. A side view shows the basic bends, but doesn't add the depth of a chair. The front view is necessary to define a complete tube.

Bending a tube is a good way to get the hang of manipulating objects in 2D and correlating the changes to the 3D model. Here's a step-by-step guide for creating a tube chair.

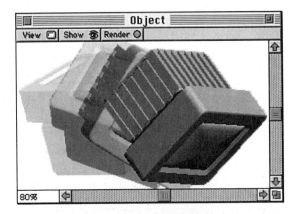

FIGURE **4.79**
Rotating objects manually or using Autospin ensures that you see an object from all angles.

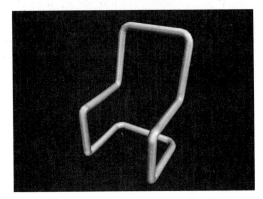

FIGURE **4.80**
A simple tube chair is made with a bent extruded tube.

1. **Open the Workshop by placing and editing the S-shaped path extrusion object**. A tube chair is basically a path extrusion object. A small, circular cross section is extruded along a chair-shaped path, creating a tube. By entering with a path extrusion object, the Workshop is set up automatically for creating path extrusions. You might want to rearrange the windows to create an alternate path extrusion layout, but leave the other settings the same. Figure 4.81 shows a useful layout for drawing this particular object.

2. **Scale the cross section down or replace it with a smaller circle.** The cross section of the default path extrusion object is a little too big for the tube chair. A cross section that's too big makes bending more difficult; the bends have a tendency to pinch when the corner is too tight.

FIGURE **4.81**

Infini-D's path extrusion layout is set up when you enter the Workshop with the S path extrusion object.

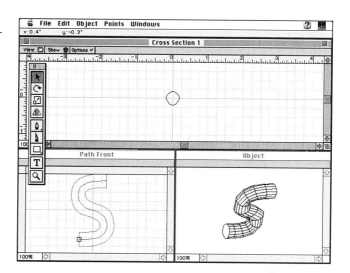

FIGURE **4.82**

A layout like this one may be better suited to building a tube chair. The larger Path view leaves more room to edit the path. The Cross Section window is smaller, because the chair has only one cross section.

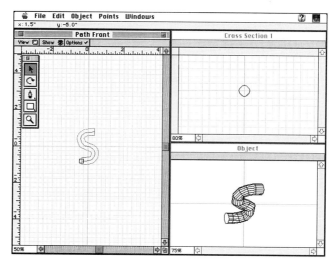

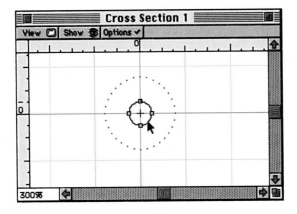

FIGURE **4.83**
Hold Shift while using the Scale tool to make the cross section smaller without distorting the proportions.

3. **Replace the path with a rounded rectangle path.** By default, rails are disabled in the path extrusion layout. So, by selecting the Rounded Rect tool from the toolbox and placing the rectangle in the

Path view, a new path is drawn. Hold the ⌘ key to automatically center the new path around the center of the grid. This is now the complete tube, which will be bent into a chair shape.

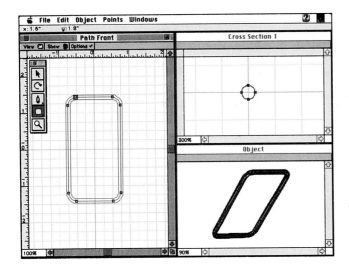

FIGURE **4.84**
Use the Rounded Rect tool to replace the path, creating the tube to be bent into the chair.

4. **Use the Pen tool to add bending points to the path.** The path must be selected first. Press the Control key to toggle the arrow. Click the path. Release the Control key and hold the Option key. The Option key enables points to be added to or removed from a path or rail. In this case, add six points to the left side of the rectangle, because each of the three necessary bends requires two points. Don't worry about the other side yet. Those points will be added later. For now, you want as few points as possible, so that the object is less confusing in the other views.

5. **Switch the Path view from front to right view.** The chair shape is defined by bending the sides of the rectangular tube.

6. **Switch visible rail pairs.** The front view displays rail pair one. When the view is switched, rail pair one lines up along the path of the object, obscuring it. The shape of the tube is not visible. Turn off rail pair one to reveal the path again and turn on rail pair two to show the tube's shape.

FIGURE **4.85**

Points are added to one side of the rectangle to facilitate bending. The other side will have points added later.

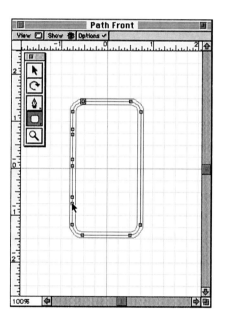

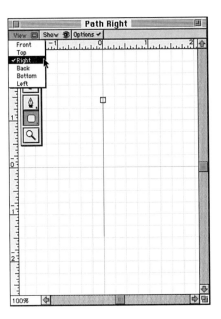

FIGURE **4.86**

Select Right from the View menu to switch viewing position.

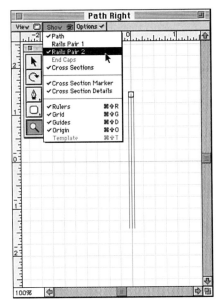

FIGURE **4.87**

Two trips to the Show menu disable rail pair one and enable rail pair two, thus revealing the path and the rail shape.

7. **Use the Arrow to drag a marquee around the top half of the object.** Although the object can be bent in any order, start with the middle bend first. Select the whole top half, all the way down the middle of the two center bend points, as shown in Figure 4.88.

8. **Use the Rotate tool to bend the tube in the middle.** The tube needs to bend at the two middle points, so place the center of rotation between them. Then, click and drag the tube down so it is horizontal. Notice that the other half of the rectangle makes a much larger radius bend. We have not yet defined bend points on the other half of the rectangle. That side is now bending out of the way, leaving us space to work on the side to which we added points. After this side is finished, you will match up the points on the other side, and the bends will be identical. During this step, you might notice that the rails seem to collapse onto the path. Don't worry about that yet. You haven't finished bending the tube, and the rails should re-expand before you're finished.

FIGURE **4.88**

Using the Arrow tool, drag a marquee around the top points.

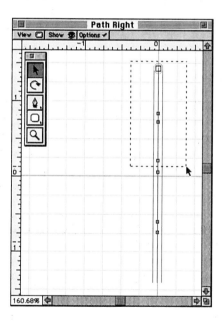

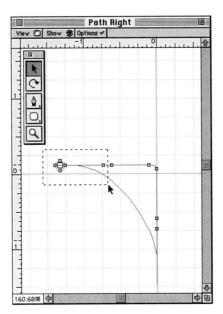

9. **Select the points for the top bend.** This time, drag the marquee around the top points, as shown in Figure 4.90.

10. **Rotate the points up to form the back of the chair.** Remember to set the centerpoint for the new bend and rotate the points up to almost vertical. The rails should re-expand at this point. Also, don't worry about the proportions of the chair seat, back, and legs yet. That can be adjusted very easily after the bends are made.

11. **Select the bottom part of the chair.** This is the last bend. Remember, select only one of the two bend points; one point stays where it is, while the other rotates.

12. **Rotate the bottom points around to form the foot of the chair.** Again, don't forget to set the centerpoint before rotating.

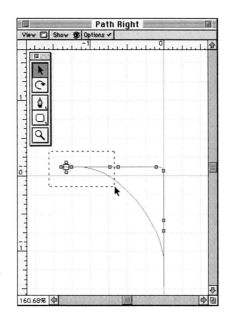

FIGURE 4.90

Drag-select the top points (which have been rotated to the left side).

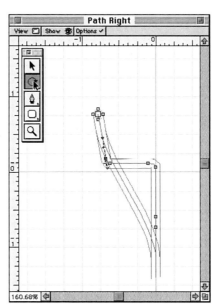

FIGURE 4.91

Rotate the selected points up to form the back of the chair.

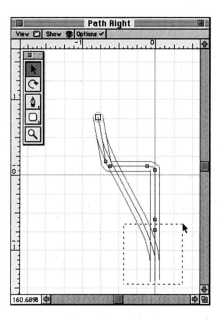

FIGURE **4.92**

For the last bend, select the bottom points.

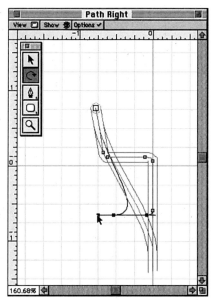

FIGURE **4.93**

The base of the chair is formed by bending the bottom of the tube.

13. Use the Pen tool to add six points to the other side of the rectangle. With one side of the chair finished, you're ready to make the other side match. You can either add the points to the exposed path, as shown in Figure 4.94, or you can switch back to the front view and add them as in step four.

14. Be sure Snap points to other points is on in the Preferences dialog. Preferences are found at the bottom of the Edit menu. Double check that this is checked on before continuing.

FIGURE **4.94**

Sizepoints are added to the opposite side of the chair using the Pen tool with the Option key pressed.

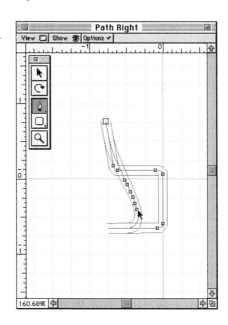

FIGURE **4.95**

Snap points to other points should be checked in the Preferences dialog.

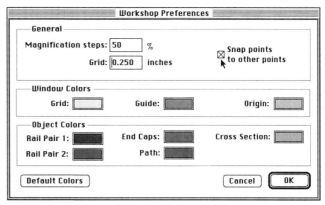

15. **Drag each new point to its corresponding point on the properly bent side.** Snap all the points into place before trying to adjust the curves. The new curves will look messy, but they're easy to fix.

16. **Select each point and use its handles to adjust the curves.** You can drag the original points out of the way. Because the new points are in the same position, you can always drag the old points back and snap them into their original positions. The curves will be restored when you move them back if you don't move the handles on the original points.

Also, you might find it useful to toggle Snap points to other points (in the Preferences dialog) off while adjusting handles. With Snap to Points on, point handles also are snapped to points, which gets in the way of fine tuning curves. Turn Snap to Points back on to move the original points back into position.

17. **Select Simplify to Pipeline from the Object menu.** Getting the rails to match takes a lot of tweaking. Simplify to Pipeline saves you that step by making the rails match the path. This step can also eliminate other problems that may have cropped up during the bending process, such as crossed rails.

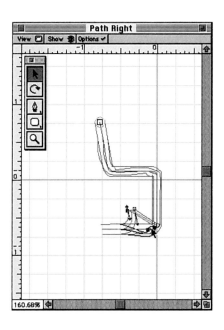

FIGURE **4.96**

Drag the six new points onto the corresponding point from the other side of the chair.

FIGURE **4.97**

Adjust the handles of the new points to match the curves of the first set of points. Move the old points out of the way if necessary.

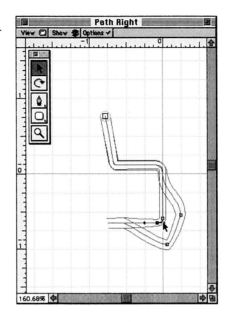

FIGURE **4.98**

Simplify to Pipeline will clean up the tube by making the rails more closely match the path.

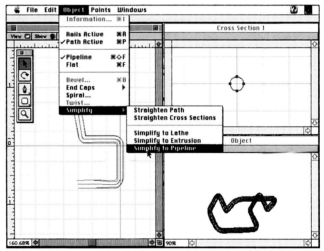

18. **Adjust the proportions of the back, seat, and legs.** Simply select the points of a particular section and drag them. Using the marquee, select points on both sides of the rectangle, keeping the sides the same. You might also want to switch back to the front view to adjust the width of the chair.

Now you have a complete tube chair frame. A seat and back can be made from separate pieces, and surfaces can be applied. Try experimenting with different window arrangements and play with adjusting handles and points. Use the Zoom tool frequently to get in closer to your work. Remember that double-clicking the Zoom tool in the Toolbox resets the window, so it's easy to get back out of a zoom.

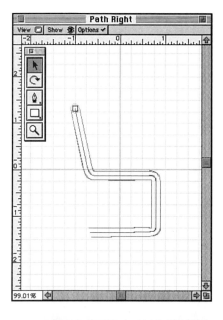

FIGURE **4.99**

Adjust the sizes of the back, seat, and legs to complete the chair. Dragging selected points in the side view selects both sides of the chair, so that movements can be made without realigning both sides.

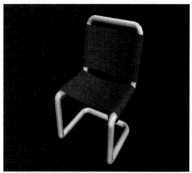

FIGURE **4.100**

Finish the chair with surfaces and the addition of a seat and back.

Spiral and Twist

Many three-dimensional shapes can be created in Infini-D's two-dimensional Workshop. There are, however, some shapes that are very difficult to build, even if you already are adept in the Workshop. For example, a spiral is quite a challenge to build in three dimensions. Twisted objects aren't so obvious either. Fortunately, Infini-D provides tools for both of these tasks.

Under the Object menu is the Spiral command. In the Spiral dialog box (see Figure 4.101), the user can enter numerical values for creating a spiral. Here's what the numbers mean.

◆ **Number of turns** is just a simple way to tell Infini-D to make a complete, 360° turn. A value of 1.000 means a single revolution. A value of 2.000 means the spiral will turn in two full circles.

◆ **Number of degrees** goes along with Number of turns to specify the number of revolutions in the spiral. As the label suggests, this setting is in degrees. Entering 360.000 is the equivalent of entering 1.000 in the Number of turns. The values of these two settings are

added, so if Number of turns is 1.000 and Number of degrees is 45.000, the spiral will turn a total of 405 degrees, or one full turn plus 45 degrees more.

◆ **Starting radius** is the distance from the center, zero on the ruler, to the starting point of the path of the spiral. A value of 1.000 makes the starting point of the spiral at one inch (or another unit if you have changed your units in the Preferences dialog) from the center of the spiral.

◆ **Ending radius** is, of course, the distance from the center of the spiral to the path at the end of the spiral. By entering different values for the starting and ending radii, the spiral can shrink or expand as it turns. The radius cannot be zero, though, so if you want a spiral that starts of ends at the center, use a very small decimal value like 0.001.

◆ **Length** determines how stretched the spiral will be. Specifically, length is the vertical distance from the starting point of the path to the ending point. This value is in inches unless the units have been changed in the Preferences dialog.

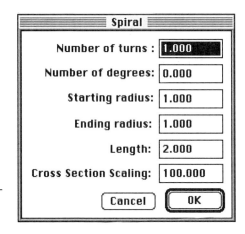

FIGURE 4.101

The Spiral dialog automates spiral creation.

◆ **Cross section Scaling** is a percentage comparison between the ending cross section and the starting cross section. The starting cross section is always the same size. The ending cross section is a percent of the size of the starting cross section. Thus, if the Cross section Scaling value is 50.000, the ending cross section will be half the size of the starting cross section. If the value is 200.000, the ending cross section will be twice the size of the first one.

TIP

Changing the shape of a spiral cross section

Every time the Spiral dialog is used, an entirely new object is built. The dialog does not modify the existing object, and it does not use any information from the existing object. That means every spiral must be built with the same cross section. Infini-D uses a

circle for the cross section, but you can change it easily.

To build a spiral with a different cross section, follow these steps.

1. **Create the spiral using the Spiral dialog.** Do this as you would normally, creating a spiral with a circular cross section.

2. **Disable Rails in the Object menu.** Rails can be visible, but they must be deactivated. If not, Infini-D will preserve the old shape, and changes to the cross section will only affect the spiral around that cross section.

3. **Edit or replace the first cross section.** The new shape will affect the whole spiral. The cross section can be replaced by any shape, including characters or text, but be sure to keep the new cross section small. If it's too big, the shape will not fit within the spiral, as shown in Figure 4.104.

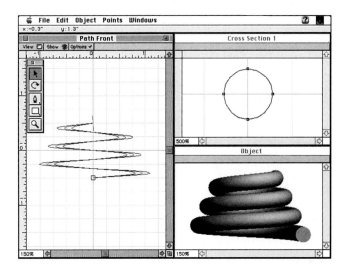

FIGURE **4.102**

A spiral made using the Spiral command automatically has a circular cross section.

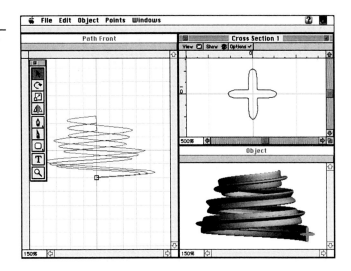

FIGURE 4.103

With rails disabled, a spiral's cross section can be replaced.

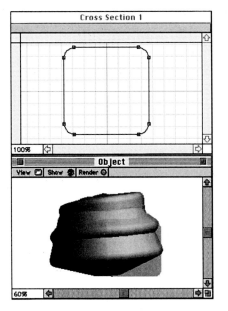

FIGURE 4.104

If the cross section is too large, the spiral overlaps itself and detail is lost.

Twisted Objects

Twisted objects are created by selecting a cross section and entering the number of degrees to twist. The twist degree is entered from the Twist item on the Object menu. After performing a twist, notice that the object's path, rails, and cross sections are unaffected. This is to avoid confusion and make modeling easier. Rather than displaying twisted rails and rotated cross sections, which quickly would get messy and difficult to see, Infini-D simply attaches a twist value to each cross section. When the object is built internally, that value is used in determining how the cross sections fit together.

FIGURE 4.105

A software box is twisted using Infini-D's Twist command.

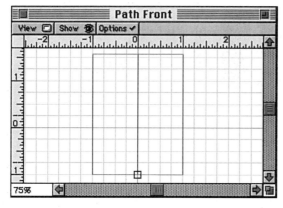

FIGURE 4.106

The rails of the box shown in Figure 4.105 are not twisted at all, making modeling easier.

There are several ways to indicate which cross section to twist.

◆ **Select a cross section from the View menu within the Cross section window.** Click the View menu and a list of all available cross sections appears. Select one you want to twist and choose Twist from the Object menu.

◆ **Click a cross section in a Path view.** With the cross section selected, choose Twist from the Object menu. One warning about selecting cross sections: because of the way Infini-D draws points, two points that are drawn over each other are not visible. Therefore, when some cross sections are selected in the Object view, there will be no apparent change to indicate the cross section is selected. This happens because each point on the cross section lines up with another point on the other side of the cross section and, when selected, the two points blank each other out. A square cross section, for example, has one point for each of its four corners. When drawn sideways, as in the Path views, the corners pair up, two on either side,

and make selections invisible. There are no adverse affects because of this behavior; there's just a little less feedback than normal.

◆ **Move the cross section marker to a cross section.** If nothing else is selected, the Twist command affects the cross section on which the cross section marker is located. Moving the cross section marker automatically deselects all points. Simply drag the cross section marker to the desired cross section and twist.

TIP
Animated twisting

Twisted objects can be animated like any other object. When the Twist command is used on a cross section that already has a twist, the current twist value is displayed in the dialog box. That value can be replaced by another, enabling objects to twist farther or to relax their twists. By editing a twisted object over time, the twist can be relaxed or tightened, creating animated twisting.

FIGURE 4.107

Twisted objects can be animated using the Sequencer.

Multiple Cross section Models

As discussed earlier, Infini-D models can have multiple cross sections. Cross sections can be any shape and have any number of points. Infini-D does its best to match up cross sections smoothly. Sometimes, however, Infini-D has some trouble matching cross sections. Here's what you can do to help smooth out transitions between cross sections.

♦ **Add more points.** Although each cross section can have any number of points, Infini-D's job is much easier if the number of points is the same. When cross sections aren't going together correctly, use the Pen tool with the Option key held down to add points to the cross sections. Adding more points will not change the shape.

♦ **Rotate the cross sections.** Sometimes rotating a cross section is enough to make the model smoother. If an object looks twisted and the number of points in each cross section is close to the same, rotating a cross section, even just a little, can help straighten things out. Rotation is most effective when the rotated cross section is either circular or when the orientation of the cross section is not important. A square cross section cannot be easily rotated, because it is very obvious where the corners are and rotation would move the corners.

TIP

Lay cross sections on top of each other to create sharp joints and forked objects.

Though Infini-D does not provide any specific controls for cross section matching, it always creates as smooth a transition as it can between two cross sections. Smooth transitions, however, are not always desired. Figure 4.108, for example, shows a square turning into a cylinder very abruptly. That kind of a joint can be made by creating, in this case, one square and a circular cross section. Then, place the two cross sections exactly on top of each other. The simplest way to line up the two cross sections is to turn on Snap points to other points in the Preferences dialog and drag the path points on top of each other. The transition happens immediately. Infini-D functions the same, but its smooth transition will not be visible.

The same trick can be used to create forked or split objects. A cross section can be two or more separate outlines, each of which defines another fork of the object. By placing cross sections on top of each other, or at least very near each other, the transition can be controlled. Then, use the rails to define the outside of the object and let the cross sections define the inside. Be careful with this method, though. When an object is split, Infini-D has to find a way to join the sides. Sometimes Infini-D chooses to join the sides in unpredictable ways.

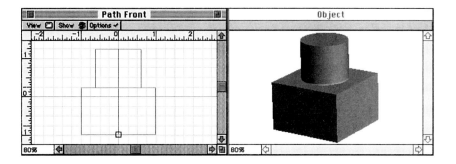

FIGURE **4.108**

The center cross section of this object is actually two cross sections laid on top of each other to create a sharp join between the sections.

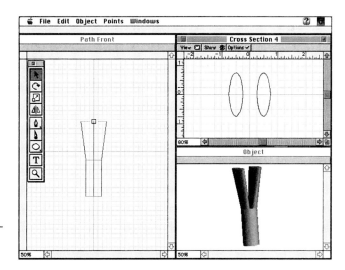

FIGURE **4.109**

Objects can be split by placing cross sections on top of each other.

Using the Object Library

In the File menu of Infini-D's Workshop, there is an item labeled Object Library. Selecting this item opens the dialog shown in Figure 4.110.

As simple as it seems, the Object Library is a powerful and useful feature. Storing models in the Library provides a quick, easy way to recall previously built models.

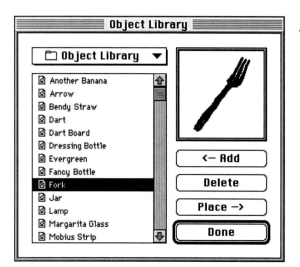

The four buttons in the Object Library are almost self-explanatory. *Add* saves the current object into the Library after prompting for a name. *Delete* removes an object from the Library. *Place* retrieves an object from the Library and places it in the Workshop. When an object is placed, however, it replaces the current model. If you're working on a model that you want to keep, add it to the Library before replacing it with a Library object. If you inadvertently replace a model you wanted to keep, there is a safety net. Click *Done* to close the Library and select Undo from the Edit menu.

Object Lesson: Morph any two objects using the Object Library

The Object Library has more advantages than just quick object recall. It enables you to morph any object into any other object very easily.

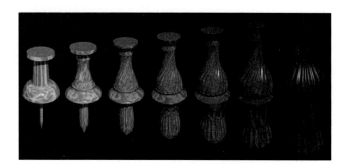

FIGURE **4.111**
Any two objects can be morphed by storing them in the Object Library.

1. **Create the second model.** This is the object into which the first will be morphed. The two models can be created in any order, but this is an efficient method that leaves little room for mistake.

2. **Store the object in the Object Library.** Infini-D will ask for a name and store the object for later use.

3. **Create the first model.**

4. **Exit the Workshop.** You now have a model ready to be morphed.

5. **Move forward in animation time.** You can move forward in time using the Snapshot command under the Animation menu or by dragging the World Time Marker in the sequencer.

6. **Reenter the Workshop with the object to be morphed (the first model, created in step 3).**

7. **Replace object one with object two.** Retrieve the second model from the Object Library. It automatically replaces the first model.

8. **Exit the Workshop.** The morph is now complete. Preview, animate, or render the sequence to see the results.

Objects stored in the Object Library are simply saved to the Object Library folder on your hard disk. If the Object Library folder is opened in the Finder, additional folders can be created using the Finder's New Folder command. Infini-D lists those folders in its Object Library dialog along with the objects. Double-clicking a folder in the Object Library dialog opens the folder to display its contents. Like a standard Open dialog, the pop-up menu at the top of the list enables you to navigate through the hierarchy of Object Library folders.

> **TIP**
>
> **Use folders to organize hierarchical models.**
>
> Infini-D's Object Library does not have the capability to store hierarchies of objects. That is, if you have a model made up of several component objects, there is no way to store that hierarchy as a single file in the Object Library. However, you can use folders to organize the parts. Simply store the parts one by one in the Library. Then, switch to the Finder and open the Object Library folder. Create a new folder, collect the parts of the object hierarchy just saved, and drop them into the new folder. This method doesn't help you reassemble the parts later, but it keeps the Object Library more organized. As objects become more complex, however, the usefulness of this method decreases, because the reassembly time becomes too great.

Object Lesson: The Golden Trumpet

One of the objects that comes with Infini-D as part of the Object Library is a single-object trumpet. This trumpet is an excellent example of using the path, rails, and cross sections together to form an object. It relies on a bent path, shape-defining rails, and multiple cross sections. Be aware, however, that this is by no means a technically accurate trumpet. For that, you'll have to get your own real trumpet to replicate in Infini-D. Here's how to construct a trumpet like the one included with Infini-D.

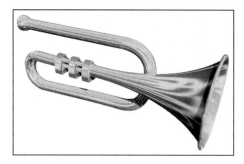

FIGURE 4.112
A single-object trumpet

1. **Select an appropriate layout.** You will change settings several times during construction, so the object type isn't important. Select one that gives you space to work. Make sure end caps are off.

2. **Place a small, circular cross section in the Cross section window.** It doesn't matter with what object you entered the Workshop. Replace the first cross section with a small circle. The rest of the object is deleted anyway.

3. **Begin the trumpet by drawing a basic path in the Path Front view.** At this point, you need a path roughly in the shape of a trumpet. Make sure nothing is selected and check that rails are deactivated. Then, use the Pen tool to define a new tube. Cross sections and rails will be taken care of later.

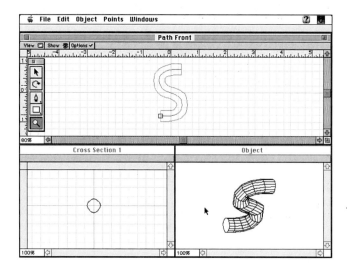

FIGURE 4.113
The wide Path view of this layout is ideal for creating a horizontally oriented trumpet.

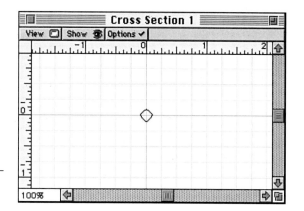

FIGURE **4.114**

*The first cross section determines the
size of most of the trumpet.*

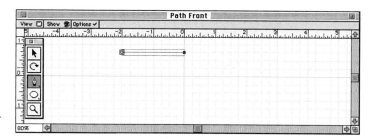

FIGURE **4.115**

Click once for each point.

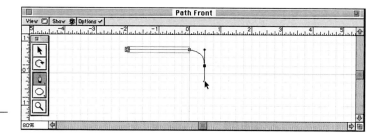

FIGURE **4.116**

Click and drag to form curve points.

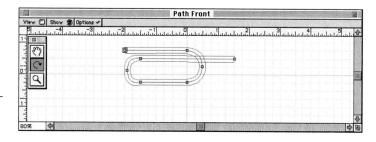

FIGURE **4.117**

*Continue all the way around to form
a basic trumpet tube as pictured here.*

4. **Switch to the Top view.** Right now, the trumpet is flat. That is, the tube curves around and goes back through itself because the path is drawn in a single plane. More dimension can be added from the Top view.

5. **Toggle the visible rails.** In the Top view, make rail pair two visible and rail pair one invisible, so that you can manipulate the path.

6. **Move the top part of the tube away from the rest of the trumpet.** It's a little tricky figuring out what point is what. The points you need to move should be easy to select, because they were drawn first. Infini-D gives selection preference to points in order of drawing. The earlier a point was drawn, the higher its selection preference. Thus, if two points are on top of each other, the one drawn first is able to be selected. Just slide the top three points up a little so that they are clear of the trumpet. Then, move the point defining the bottom of the first curve up a little so that the tube becomes a diagonal along the bottom of the trumpet. See Figures 4.118–4.121 for more direction.

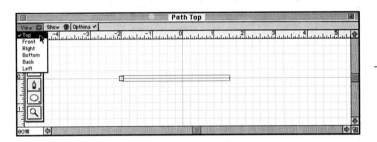

FIGURE 4.118

The View menu within the Path view is used to switch views. Switch to the Top view to add depth to the trumpet.

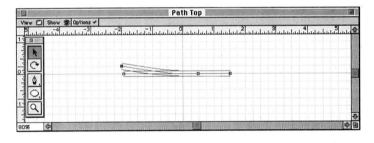

FIGURE 4.119

Select and drag the starting point of the path up so it is clear of the tube below.

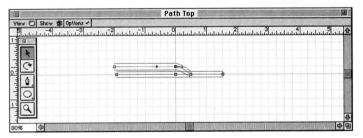

FIGURE 4.120

Select the second point on the path and drag it upward in-line with the first point. Snap to Grid is useful for keeping the tube straight.

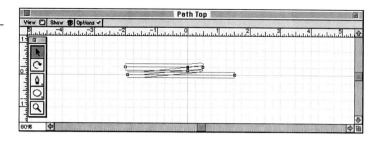

FIGURE **4.121**

Drag the third point up in-line with the first two. Finally, drag the fourth point up about halfway to the other three points. This last point is at the bottom of the first curve in the Front view. In the Top view, that means it will be wrapped back underneath the tube slightly.

7. **Switch back to the Front view.** Remember to toggle the rails again.

8. **Make any necessary adjustments to the Front view of the tube.** Sometimes adjustments in the Top view cause changes in the front or side views. Make these changes now before you modify the rails and cross sections.

9. **Simplify to Pipeline.** Now is the last chance to use this time-saving feature.

Using the Simplify to Pipeline command cleans up the rails by matching them with the path. Later, when the rails and path won't match, using the command removes any changes made to the rails.

10. **Zoom in on the start of the path.** You're ready to create a mouthpiece for the trumpet. Use the Zoom tool to drag a rectangle around the start of the path. Infini-D enlarges that rectangle to fill the screen.

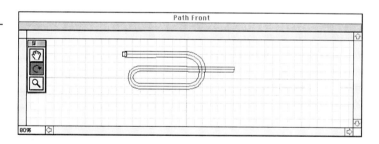

FIGURE **4.122**

While working in the Top view, the front may get distorted. Readjust it so it looks like this. You might need to toggle back and forth between the two views to tweak it just right.

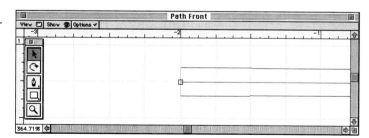

FIGURE **4.123**

Zoom in on the mouth of the tube. Fine adjustments are much easier when the view is enlarged.

11. **Make sure Mirror 4-way is on.** Before making changes to a rail, turn Mirror 4-way on, so that the rails all reflect the changes and maintain the tube shape.

12. **Hold the Option key and click the path just after the first point.** The rails should bulge a little for the mouthpiece, so add an extra point to the path. Rail points are created automatically.

13. **Drag one of the rail end points up to form a small cone.**

14. **Change the point type to curve.**

15. **Drag a handle out of the point to form a curve.**

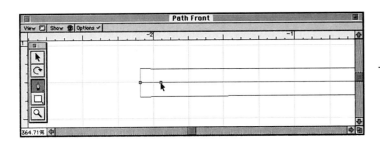

FIGURE **4.124**
Hold the Option key and use the Pen tool to click the path. This makes room for the rails to bulge at the beginning.

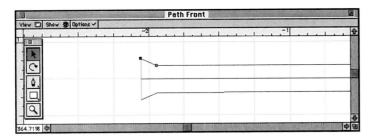

FIGURE **4.125**
Drag an end point up to form a cone. The other rails mirror the change.

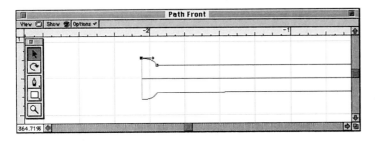

FIGURE **4.126**
Drag a handle out of the end point to form the curve of the mouthpiece.

16. **Select the first path point.**

17. **Use the Pen tool to add an additional path point before the original first point.**

18. **Change the new point's type to curve.**

19. **Drag the new point down and use the handles to drag out a curve.** This curve wraps around to give the mouthpiece the appearance of thickness. Once the curve is made, the mouthpiece is complete. Figure 4.128 shows the Path view of the completed mouthpiece.

20. **Double-click the Zoom tool to reset the Path view zoom level.**

21. **Show the cross section marker if it is hidden.** The cross section marker is the small square that slides along the path when dragged. Often, it is useful to hide the cross section marker in order to get at the path. If you have done so, show the marker again now.

22. **Drag the cross section marker to the top of the second curve.** Place the next cross section here. Make sure to line the cross section marker up with the point that is already at the top of this curve. Otherwise, you'll create extra points.

23. **Insert a cross section.** In the Options menu, select Insert Cross section. This cross section is inserted to ensure that the rails maintain their proper shape. You might find it useful to insert other cross sections to maintain the rail shape, but it is not usually necessary.

FIGURE **4.127**

With the path point associated with that cross section, a click with the Pen tool adds a new point before the original start of the path.

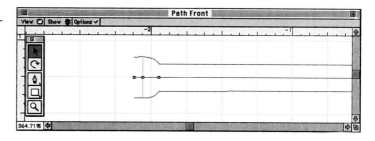

FIGURE **4.128**

Use the point's handles to define a curve wrapping around inside the tube. Be careful not to intersect the cross section. Infini-D doesn't behave well when rails pass through a cross section.

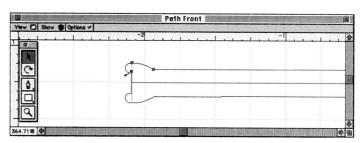

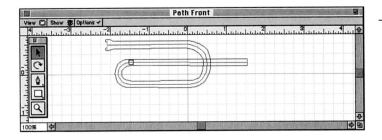

FIGURE **4.129**

Drag the cross section marker to the top of the second curve, as shown here, and let it snap onto the point already there.

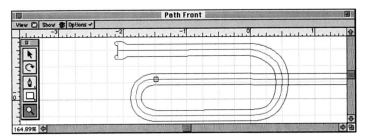

FIGURE **4.130**

Insert a cross section here to help the rails maintain their shape.

24. **Drag the cross section marker forward along the path.**

25. **Add another cross section.** This cross section and the previous one should both be the same as the original circular cross section.

26. **Drag the cross section marker forward again.**

26. **Add another cross section.** This is the first part of the trumpet's valves.

27. **Turn off mirroring.** Select Mirror None. The changes to the cross sections at this point should not be mirrored.

27. **Switch to the Cross section view.**

28. **Replace the circular cross section with a valve-like cross section.** Often, the path will twist slightly as a result of the curves. If this is the case, you might have to rotate the cross section to orient it correctly on the trumpet. Alternatively, you can clean up the path and rails to keep them from

twisting. Adding more cross sections can help this process.

29. **In the Path view, drag the path point associated with the new valve cross section onto the previous circular cross section.** The two cross sections together create a sharp joint.

30. **Drag the cross section marker forward and add a new cross section.** The new cross section determines the thickness of the valve, so place it accordingly. At this point, it is helpful to disable the rails from the Object menu, so that Infini-D will use the new shape entirely and will not preserve the circular cross section shape.

31. **Add another cross section farther along the path.**

32. **In the Cross section view, replace the new cross section with two circles.** You might have to rotate the cross section to orient it between the valves.

FIGURE **4.131**

Insert a second cross section. This
controls the joint between the tube
and the valve.

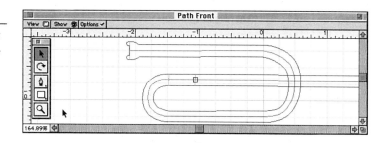

FIGURE **4.132**

Replace the round cross section with a
valve-shaped cross section. Rotate it as
needed to match the orientation of
the trumpet. This cross section was
rotated counterclockwise by
approximately 50°.

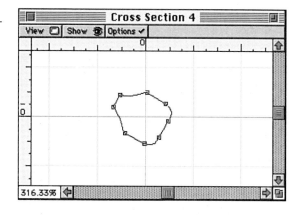

FIGURE **4.133**

The new valve cross section is dragged
back on top of the previous cross
section. In this picture, the cross
section under the cross section marker
is actually the two cross sections
lined up.

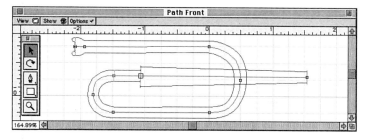

FIGURE **4.134**

The trumpet splits into two small
tubes at this point. The cross section is
drawn as two separate circles.

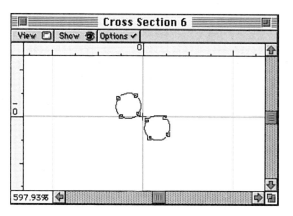

33. **In the Path view, drag the new cross section back on top of the previous cross section.** The joint between the valve and the split tubes will be much cleaner.

34. **Insert another cross section.** This is the end of the split tube section.

35. **Insert another cross section.** Start a new valve.

36. **Copy and paste a valve cross section into the new cross section.** This valve should look identical to the first one, so use the View menu to switch cross sections. Select the outline and choose Copy from the Edit menu. Switch back to the new cross section and choose Paste from the Edit menu. Delete any outlines left from the cross section Infini-D automatically inserted.

37. **Move the new valve cross section back on top of the previous split cross section.** The joint is now cleaner.

38. **Repeat steps 30–37 to finish this valve, make another split tube segment, and begin a third valve.** Copy and paste where necessary to keep identical cross sections for the repeating sections.

39. **Repeat step 30 to close the third valve.**

40. **Insert another cross section.**

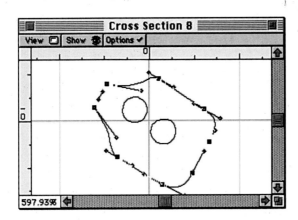

FIGURE 4.135

Copy and paste one of the valve cross sections onto the new cross section. Delete the two circles that Infini-D created when the cross section was inserted.

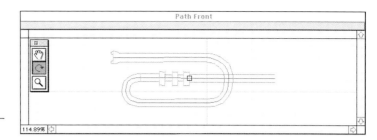

FIGURE 4.136

Trumpet cross section

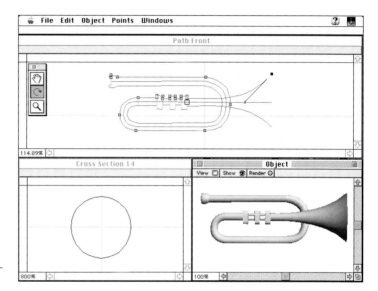

FIGURE 4.137

Trumpet

Surfaces

Even the most complex models and smoothest animation are somewhat bland without good surfaces. Infini-D's default surface is White Plastic. Although adequate, an entire scene in White Plastic is not very exciting. Fortunately, Infini-D has some very powerful surfacing features.

FIGURE 5.1

The Surface Info dialog provides many controls for creating an infinite variety of surfaces, including wood, marble, glass, fractals, and many others.

Surface Properties

An Infini-D surface is made up of several basic components. Like creating a recipe, these components can be blended together in countless different ways to create an infinite variety of different surfaces.

Diffuse Shading: Defines how much a surface reflects or absorbs light. A Diffuse Shading component of 0% absorbs all light and appears black. A Diffuse Shading component of 100% reflects all light. Diffuse Shading affects the intensity of color. A blue surface, for example, becomes a darker shade of blue as you lower the Diffuse Shading component.

Specular Highlight: A Specular Highlight is the reflection of light off an object, such as a white dot on a billiard ball or an eyeball. A Specular Highlight component of 0% reflects no light at all. A Specular Highlight component of 100% reflects light at the fullest intensity. The color of the Specular Highlight is the color of the light. A green light, for example, creates a green specular highlight.

Shininess: The Shininess affects the size of the Specular Highlight. A Shininess factor of 0% makes a diffuse, larger Specular Highlight. A Shininess factor of 100% creates a tight, small Specular Highlight.

Metallicity: The Metallicity component affects how much of an object's surface color is added to the color of the Specular Highlight. Metallic objects tend to reflect a specular highlight that is the color of their surface. Copper, for example, tends to reflect an orange-red specular highlight. With a Metallicity factor of 0%, the color of the specular highlight is the color of the light. A metallicity factor of 100%, on the other hand, combines the color of the light and the color of the surface.

Glow: Glow affects the intensity of the surface color, making it appear as if illuminated from within. A Glow setting of 0% makes the surface of the object appear normal (no change). A Glow setting of 100% increases the intensity of the object's surface color, giving the appearance of a neon or glowing object.

Reflectiveness: The amount that the surface reflects either other objects (ray tracing) or an environment map (shading). In ray tracing mode, a given point on an object's surface is a combination of the object's surface color and the color of the object it is reflecting. In shading mode, the point is a combination of the surface color and the color of the environment map. In both cases, 0% reflectiveness shows just the color of the surface. A 100% reflectiveness is a full combination of the reflected object or environment map and the surface's color.

Transparency: The amount that an object lets light pass through it. A somewhat transparent object will let some light through, displaying objects behind the surface. The color of the object depends on the surface properties (color, diffuse shading, etc.), the degree of transparency, and the color of the background showing through the object. 0% transparency lets no light through; 100% transparency makes the object fully transparent. (Note: Only works with ray tracing.)

Index of Refraction: Light bends as it travels through a transparent object. Making the Index of Refraction higher or lower causes light to bend. An Index of Refraction of 1.0 has no bending whatsoever. Infini-D can handle Indices of Refraction ranging from 0.50 to 5.50, which correspond to real-world values. For more information on Indices of Refraction, see Appendix A. (Note: Only works with ray tracing.)

Figures 5.2-5.5
Diffuse shading

Figures 5.6-5.9
Specular highlight

Figures 5.10-5.13
Shininess

Figures 5.14-5.17
Metallicity

Figures 5.18-5.21
Glow

Figures 5.22-5.25
Reflectiveness

Figures 5.26-5.29
Transparency

FIGURE **5.30**

Indices of Refraction, 0.85

FIGURE **5.31**

1.00

FIGURE **5.32**

1.10

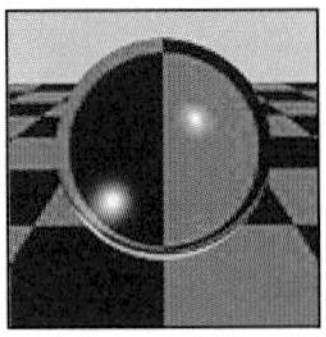

FIGURE **5.33**

1.65

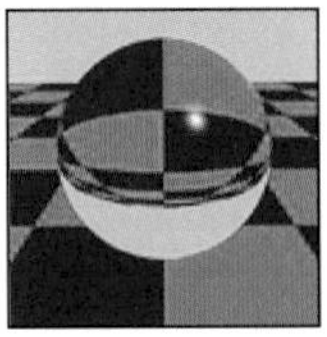

FIGURE **5.34**

5.50

Procedural Surfaces

A *procedural surface* simply means that a surface is defined mathematically, instead of using a PICT (texture) map. Infini-D completes a mathematical procedure, or algorithm, to create the surface.

If you want to create a marble vase, for example, you have two options: use Infini-D's procedural marble, or use a scanned texture map of marble.

FIGURE 5.35

The object on the left uses a mathematically defined procedural marble, which saves disk space and RAM, and also is modifiable. The object on the right uses a PICT image of marble, trading increases in disk and RAM usage for improvements in surface quality.

The advantage of using procedural surfaces is that they take up less memory and disk space than texture maps, and are stored inside the Infini-D scene file, so that you don't have to keep the texture maps in the same folder. The disadvantage of using procedural surfaces is that they are generally slower than using texture maps.

There are many types of procedural surfaces within Infini-D. Here are the different types and some recommendations for using them.

Flat Color: Also known as a *homogenous surface*, this defines a surface with a single uniform color, such as paper or plastic. Although a flat color is defined by a single RBG color, the color might not appear uniformly across the object, depending on lighting and the Diffuse component of the surface itself.

Note that the homogeneity only applies to the appearance of color in the surface. A surface can still have attributes, such as bumpiness or corrosion, that affect appearance and how the surface represents the color component.

Mandelbrot set: Discovered by Benoit Mandelbrot of Yale University, the Mandelbrot set is an iterating function operating on a grid of complex and imaginary numbers. The function is fed a *seed*, and the amount of time it takes to escape the function determines the color of the point being calculated. This simple algorithm yields fantastic swirls of color and shape, which are, in theory, infinitely complex. You can zoom into any portion of a Mandelbrot set to get more detail. This mathematical tie-dye creates patterns that are both intricate and beautiful.

To use the Mandelbrot set, drag a marquee around a section of the fractal and use the Magnifying Glass buttons to zoom in and out. The two colors set the boundaries of the *escape function*. A little known trick, rather than just doing a standard surface cross-fade, is to set two surfaces with different Mandelbrot sets and let Infini-D interpolate or morph between the two fractals.

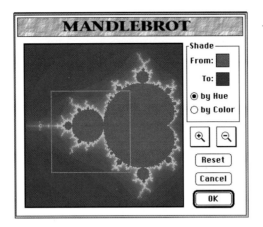

FIGURE 5.36

The Mandelbrot dialog controls the colors and zoom level of the fractal surface.

Julia set: The Julia set is an offshoot of the Mandelbrot set; it uses a point inside the Mandelbrot set for the seed that creates a new, symmetrical fractal. Like the Mandelbrot set, the Julia set can be animated, or morphed, by applying two different Julia sets to an object at different times. The capability to animate the seed, or point in the Mandelbrot set, adds a delicious new element of complexity to the animation.

Julia sets are particularly useful for creating planetary effects, and are also great for creating 3D terrain. (See Chapter 8, "Terrains.")

Tiling: The Tiling box lets users choose interlocking, Escher-style tiles for creating anything from checkerboards to zoot-suit patterns. Each odd or even tile can be set to a different surface. You could have, for example, a checkerboard with alternating mirror and marbled squares.

The Tile dialog box enables you to create interesting, interlocking tile patterns. Moving a point on one side of the tile causes the adjacent point on the opposite side to move as well. This method makes sure that any tile you create interlocks seamlessly.

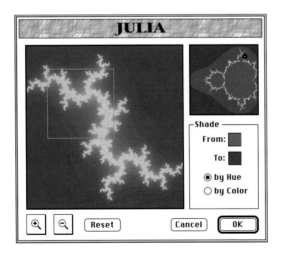

FIGURE 5.37

The Julia set dialog works like the Mandelbrot dialog: define a square with the mouse and click the Magnifier tool buttons to zoom in and out. The Mandelbrot image in the upper right corner determines which part of the Mandelbrot set is used to form the Julia set for the surface.

FIGURE 5.38

Tiled surfaces are edited in the Tile dialog. The shape is defined by dragging points around the grid on the right, and surfaces are chosen from the pop-up menus at the top.

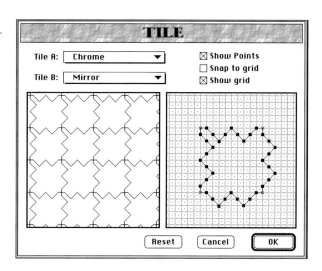

TIP

For precise alignment, turn off Snap to Grid.

Despite the suggestive name, Snap to Grid doesn't do as good a job as you might think. If tiles need to be neat and clean, line up the points by hand. Believe it or not, you'll do a better job lining up points using the visible grid than Infini-D will do trying to line them up using its internal grid.

Noise: Noise, marble, wood, and natural wood are dependent on the principle of a *noise lattice*. Imagine a three-dimensional noise pattern, as if you had a pool filled with colored oils of different densities. This is a noise lattice. To create a *noise pattern*, Infini-D dunks your object into this virtual noise pattern, creating a unique surface pattern.

Adjusting the Density slider adjusts the size of the noise map relative to your object. A high density creates a tight, grainy noise pattern, whereas a low density creates a loose, swirling pattern. The *from* and *to* colors determine the color range of your noise gradient. Choosing *By Color* interpolates between the RGB values of the colors you have selected. Choosing *By Hue* interpolates by hue, finding the closest path around the perimeter of the classic color circle.

FIGURE 5.39

The Noise dialog sets the density and color for a noise surface. Select By Hue to create psychedelic noise patterns.

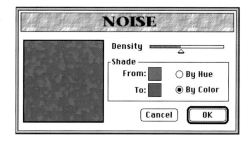

Marble: Marble is a variant of the noise gradient, with some additional parameters available for creating a marble-like appearance. The X, Y, and Z weights determine the strength of the noise lattice along the X, Y, and Z parameters. In a sense, think of these parameters in terms of the respective influence that the width, height, and depth will have on your pool of colored oils.

Turbulence determines the amount of noise in your noise lattice. A low turbulence value creates a smoother, less veined marble. A high turbulence value creates a more complex, veined marble.

Cohesion determines how much the colors clump together. A high cohesion factor has bigger blocks of color, whereas a low cohesion factor has smaller areas of color. The two colors you select in the dialog box determine the range of color within your marble.

Wood/Natural Wood: Infini-D's woods are variants of the noise lattice. The Swirl, Grain, and Cut parameters in Wood determine the characteristics of the X, Y, and Z components of the wood and the color range.

Natural wood is more sophisticated than Wood, offering a variety of parameters. The Cut parameters (Radial, Tangential, and Cross Section) determine how the wood is oriented relative to your object. The Radius, Ring Scale, and Gnarliness parameters determine the size, scale, and cohesion of the rings within the wood, respectively.

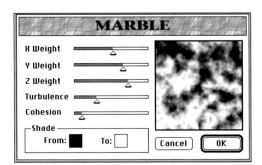

FIGURE **5.40**

The Marble dialog creates a number of different surfaces, from veined marbles to clouds to cow spot patterns.

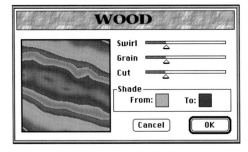

FIGURE **5.41**

Wood is a basic procedural surface type that creates simple, grained patterns.

FIGURE 5.42

Natural Wood provides more options and greater control than Wood, and, accordingly, creates much more realistic wood patterns.

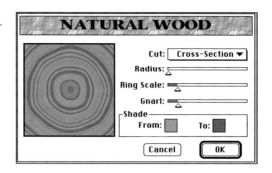

Infini-D also has several ways to modify the different types of procedural surfaces. These effects are forms of *bump maps*. That is, they are all methods for adding depth to surfaces with various bump types. The three surface effects are as follows.

Wave: The Wave function enables you to create sinusoidal waves that run along objects.

Combined with a reflective surface, such as a mirror or water, waves can add a beautifully realistic element to a ray traced scene. Waves also can be animated. The Wave parameters, such as the amplitude and decay of the wave, can be animated, and the Wave dialog enables the user to set the number of waves per second and the direction of wave flow in an animation.

FIGURE 5.43

Waves are edited and animated in the Wave dialog. Multiple waves can be added and combined, each with its own height, decay, and speed.

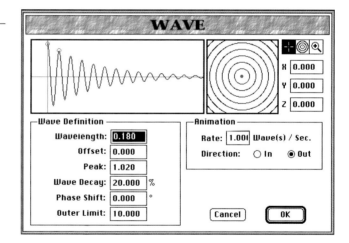

Offset waves if effect is not visible.

Some objects won't display waves correctly. A default wave applied to a sphere, for example, will not be visible. There are two ways to make the waves visible.

◆ **Offset the wave by dragging it from the center of the Wave dialog.** The X and Y values of the wave position are affected, and the wave should appear. The wave, however, will no longer be centered on the object.

◆ **Change the Z value.** The wave appears centered on the X and Y axes and, thus, centered on the object. The side effect is that the wave is not centered on the sides of other objects. A cube, for example, won't have the wave applied to all sides. The vertical sides are not centered.

Bump/Corrosion: Bumps and corrosion work by applying a bumpiness, based on a noise pattern, to an object's surface. Controlling the density of the bumps affects the appearance of the surface. A very bumpy texture looks like granite, especially with a good deal of specular highlight, and a slightly bumpy texture looks like stone. A corroded surface is basically an inverse bump; however, this subtle distinction often can make a big difference. Coal, for example, looks better with a dense corrosion than a bump.

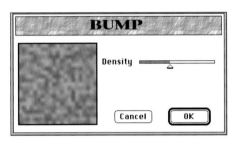

FIGURE 5.44

The Bump dialog is basically grayscale noise that gives the effect of raised markings on a surface.

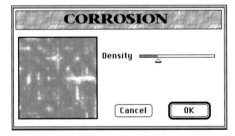

FIGURE 5.45

Corrosion works the opposite of bumps, cutting into a surface instead of bumping out of it.

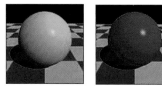

FIGURES 5.50-5.53
Mandelbrot set, interpolating 1

FIGURES 5.54-5.57
Julia, interpolating 1

FIGURES 5.58-5.62
Tile

FIGURES 5.63-5.67
Noise 1

FIGURES **5.68-5.72**

Marble 1

FIGURE **5.73**

Wood 1

FIGURE **5.74**

Wood 2

FIGURES **5.75-5.77**

Natural Wood

FIGURES **5.78-5.82**

Wave

FIGURES **5.83-5.85**

Bump

Composed Surfaces

Infini-D's most powerful surfacing capabilities are found in the Surface Composition dialog. Surface composition combines any number of procedural surfaces and imagemaps. In addition to several reveal methods and wrapping modes, component surfaces can be used as highlight maps, bump maps, reflection maps, transparency maps, or glow maps. Surface components can be arranged on an object also, enabling precise alignment of multiple images on a single object.

To create a composed surface, select an object and choose Compose Surface from the Object menu. The Surface Composition dialog, shown in figure 5.88, appears with White Plastic as a layer. Double-click the White Plastic

layer to replace it with another surface (click the Add Layer button to add another layer without replacing White Plastic). Select a surface from the surface list or click the Get Image button to load a PICT image or QuickTime movie. Click OK. The surface or image is imported as a layer in the composed Surface Library.

By default, images and surfaces are imported as layers with the Surface slider checked. This means that all color information is used as a surface. The slider represents what percentage of the surface is used. So, to combine surface layers, add two or more layers and set their surface percentages to less than 100. The surfaces will then blend together.

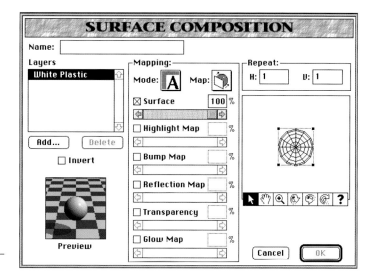

FIGURE 5.88

The Surface Composition dialog

For all other properties (highlight, bump, reflection, transparency, and glow), only the gray levels are used. Any black in the image is affected by whichever property is being used, while white is left alone. Levels of gray are used as in-between levels. The surface is more affected in the darker gray areas. Grayscale images are ideal, because you can see exactly what information Infini-D uses. Color images can be used as well, but Infini-D ignores the color information and just uses the intensity (Infini-D basically turns the image into grayscale).

Position layers using the toolset at the bottom right of the Composition dialog. In the box above the toolset, the current layer is represented by a rectangle. Each corner of the rectangle is a draggable point. The Arrow tool moves the layer and dragging a corner scales the layer. The Rotate tools spin the object being surfaced (a sphere, if nothing was selected when entering the Compose Surface dialog). Imagine that you are holding a sticker or decal in your hands and have an object on which to place the sticker. The natural way to make the placement is to hold the sticker facing you and rotate the object. When you find the area for the sticker, it is dropped straight onto the object. Infini-D's surface positioning tools work the same way.

Clicking the button labeled with a question mark presents a dialog for precise numerical alignment of surfaces, if manual alignment is not accurate enough. The most important feature of this dialog is the Align With pop-up menu. Selecting a surface layer from this menu exactly aligns the current surface with the selected surface. If you have matching bump and color maps, use Align With to drop them precisely on top of each other. Note that Align With does not lock the two layers. If you move one layer, use Align With to match up the surfaces again.

Finally, it's important to know the order of the layers in the Layers list. The topmost layer in the list is actually the bottom of the surface layer stack. As new layers are added, they are listed below the previous layers. That's because Infini-D adds new layers on top of old layers, and, in the Layers list, that means the new layers show up at the bottom of the list. It's a little confusing at first, but it doesn't take long to get used to.

TIP

Place surface effect maps on top of surface color maps.

A composed surface consisting of a color, or surface, layer, and a bump map should be ordered with the bump on top of the surface (which means the bump should appear below the surface layer in the Layers list). That way, the surface layer is used for color, the bump map is on top of that, and the bump then affects the color below it. If the order is reversed, the bump is applied to a blank surface, and the surface map will cover up the bump, leaving a flat-looking surface. This ordering procedure applies to all composed surface effects, including reflectivity, glow, highlight, and transparency.

Using Decals

Decal is a method for applying composed surface layers to objects. A decal layer behaves as if it were pinned onto the object. As the object bends and twists, the surface bends and twists with it. There are a few aspects of decal usage that are important to understand.

First, decals cannot be applied to the end caps of an object. Basically, a decal can only be applied to the part of an object that is defined by rails. Thus, if the rails are folded in on the ends to form rail-based end caps, decals can be applied. Alternatively, a separate layer can be applied to the end caps. If the decal layer is laid on top of the end cap layer, the two layers should mix cleanly.

Next, you should know how to work the sliders labeled "H" and "V" that appear when decal is the chosen mapping method. As the labels imply, the H slider controls the horizontal placement of the decal and the V slider controls the vertical placement. The wireframe model above the sliders displays the sliders' effects by way of green and red lines representing the edges of the decal. Move the sliders around a bit to see how the decal changes. The rotation controls, in this case, are only provided for viewing the decaled object from different angles; they have no effect on the position of the surface. While there is no free rotation control for decals, there are some orientation controls available by clicking the question mark button.

Finally, the decal sets a size and position for a single copy of the image being placed. You can still use the repeat values, however, to replicate the decal. Setting the H repeat to 3, for example, will copy the decal three times and place the copies horizontally around the object. To repeat the decal indefinitely, press Delete. An infinity symbol will appear to indicate an infinite repeat.

FIGURE 5.89

Decals are applied in the rectangle defined by the lines in the wireframe view on the right. The effect is visible in the preview on the left.

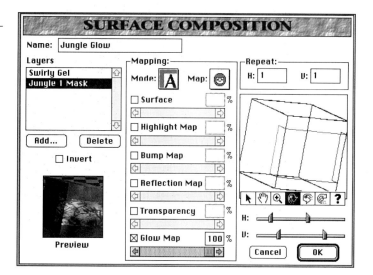

Object Lesson: Composing a Billiard Ball

A billiard ball is a simple composed surface that demonstrates how composed surfaces are made. Here's how to make an eight ball.

1. **Create a surface map in a paint program.** Use a paint or drawing program, such as Photoshop or Illustrator, to create a surface map. The map should be a black square with a white circle on it. In the center of the circle is a black number eight. Save this file as a PICT file.

2. **Make a highlight and reflection map.** Again, use a paint or drawing program. In this case, the image should be a plain black square. Just erase the circled eight from the first image if you like, but be sure to do a

Save As so you don't save over the original. Making a plain black square for part of a surface might seem strange, but it does make sense. The ball needs to be shiny and reflective over the entire surface. Within a composed surface, the only way to do that is with a solid color. If we used gray instead of black, the entire surface would be less shiny and less reflective. However, instead of worrying about getting the gray exactly right in another program, we'll just use the sliders in the Compose dialog to set the highlight and reflective values.

T**IP**

Highlights and reflections cover the entire object uniformly when a black square is used for the highlight and reflection maps.

FIGURE **5.90**
The Eight Ball

FIGURE **5.91**
The surface map looks something like this.

3. **In Infini-D, place a sphere.** This is your eight ball.

4. **Select Compose Surface from the Render menu.** Infini-D opens the Surface Composition dialog, and you're ready to put everything together.

5. **Double-click the White Plastic layer.** No white plastic is needed for the eight ball, so replace it.

6. **Get Image and import the surface map.** The surface value should be left at 100%, because this is the surface layer. Straight mapping is correct as well. The surface is mapped through the object and an eight appears on both sides.

7. **Click the Question Mark button and enter -90 for the X rotation value.** The eight is then mapped properly onto the side of the ball.

8. **Click the Add button and import the highlight/reflection map.** If you're following these steps in order, the layers are now in the correct order. If not, swap them so the surface layer is at the top of the list (and, thus, the bottom of the surface layers stack).

9. **Check off the surface map for the highlight/reflection map layer.** Otherwise, the black layer will cover the eights and you'll only have a large black sphere.

10. **Check highlight map.** Set the slider at 100%.

11. **Check reflection map.** Set the slider to 40%. An eight ball shouldn't be a mirror, but it is somewhat reflective. Adjust this value to your liking.

12. **Give the surface a name and click OK.**

Shade-Best or ray trace the ball to see the new surface. It might be difficult to see on a black background, but the eight ball should look good on the green felt of a pool table. If the ball is a little too dark, edit the composed surface and select the highlight/reflection layer. Check Glow on and set it to a low value, such as 15%. That way the ball is just a touch brighter, without actually looking like it is lit.

Use Parent's Surface

At the top of Infini-D's Apply Surface submenu (under the Render menu) is a single item separated from the others by a line. That item is labeled *Use Parent's Surface* and has to do with linked objects. When two or more objects are linked, they can share a surface. There are several reasons to use a parent object's surface on a child.

◆ **Procedural surfaces can span multiple objects.** Because procedural surfaces are computed as a *surface space*, multiple objects can be placed in the same procedural surface. The result is a continuing pattern across several objects. To use the same surface on multiple objects, link the objects to a parent. Select Use Parent's Surface for the children and apply a procedural surface to the parent.

◆ **Easier surface changes later.** If a hierarchy of objects all use the same surface, there is no need to change each object's surface.

Simply apply a surface to the parent object (even an invisible parent), and then select Use Parent's Surface for each child object. Now, when changes need to be made, change the Parent's Surface, and children's objects reflect the change.

Animation Assistants

Suppose you want to take advantage of Use Parent's Surface, but the object hierarchy is already built. It would be tedious at best to select each object in turn and apply the surface. Animation Assistants can help, even if you're not making an animation. Follow these steps:

1. **Open the Sequencer.**

2. **Select the parent object by clicking the name.**

3. **Hold the Option key down and click the triangle to the left of the object name.** Clicking the triangle expands the first level of the object hierarchy, but because the Option key is pressed, the entire hierarchy expands at all levels.

4. **Select the eventmarks of all objects to be surfaced.** Drag a marquee around the eventmarks, or use the Shift key to select multiple eventmarks.

5. **Choose the Apply Surface at Eventmarks Animation Assistant from the Animation menu.**

6. **Select Use Parent's Surface.** Any surface can be selected, and this is a good method for applying surfaces to any object hierarchy. In this case, we want to select Use Parent's Surface so we only have to do the process once. After Use Parent's Surface is selected, there is no need to apply a surface to each of the children.

Object Lesson: Building a Home: Modeling Earth

For obvious reasons, the Earth and Earth-like planets are commonly modeled objects. There are several effective ways to model Earth-like planets. Here are a few different tips for building planets.

◆ **Use layers of marble patterns to simulate earth and water.** Earth-like planets can be built completely within Infini-D using procedural marbles. A green and blue marble with a fairly dense bump creates a good looking planet, although marble's two-color limitation *does* decrease surface detail.

◆ **Use an imagemap of a real planet.** Earth photographs aren't hard to find. If you have a good scan of the earth, without too many clouds, use it on a sphere to create a realistic earth. A grayscale version of the same photograph can be used as a bump map to give the planet a rough surface.

◆ **Use a second sphere as a cloud layer.** Rather than composing a single surface, put the clouds on a second, slightly larger sphere around the planet. That way, the clouds are raised off the surface of the planet and will create shadows on the surface when ray traced.

FIGURE 5.92

A marble surface with bumps or corrosion can provide an acceptable planet surface, especially when clouds are added.

FIGURE 5.93

The map image from the System Scrapbook can be used as an earth surface.

◆ **Use a transparency map on a white sphere for the clouds.** Infini-D's marble makes a good cloud cover if a black and white marble is used as a transparency layer in a composed surface. Alternatively, a transparency map can be made in Photoshop, or another paint program, and imported. Infini-D's marbles have one advantage, however, in that they can be morphed. Several different marbles combined make excellent animated clouds.

FIGURE 5.94

A layer of clouds can add immeasurable depth and quality to any planet. Use a separate sphere with a transparency map for clouds.

Object Lesson: Falling Water: Making Water Droplets

Creating an animated water ripple in Infini-D is fairly straightforward; just apply a wave and set the number of waves per second. But what if you want to start with a smooth surface, drop something into it, and have the surface respond with a ripple?

1. **Create the flat surface.** This is the surface in its normal, unrippled state.

2. **Add a wave.** The first of three different waves, this wave should be small. Make the peak value 0 so that the wave is invisible. Set the waves per second to 3 and make sure the direction is set to *out*. Think of this as applying a potential wave. The surface remains flat at this point, but the wave is there, waiting to happen.

3. **Duplicate the surface.**

4. **Set the peak value of the new surface to 1.000.** The ripple is now in full swing, so that the waves are at their highest point.

5. **Duplicate the second wave.**

6. **Change the offset of the new wave to 1.000.** The center of the droplet spreads out, leaving a smooth surface behind.

7. **Set the peak value to 0 again.** The wave fades away as the ripples spread out.

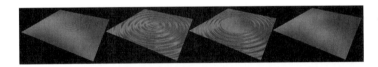

FIGURE 5.95
A water droplet

FIGURE 5.96
Start with a flat surface.

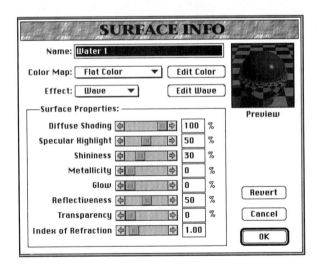

FIGURE 5.97

*Add wave potential by making a
small wave.*

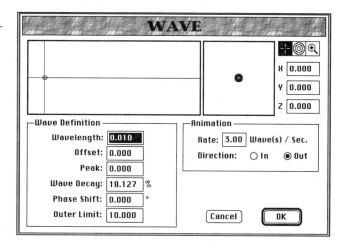

FIGURE 5.98

*The ripple reaches its peak in the
second wave.*

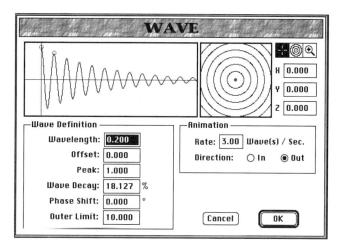

You end up with three separate wave surfaces. Now, to make a droplet, simply assign the three waves, in order and over time, to an object. You can do so using the Snapshot command under the Animation menu, or with the Sequencer; just move forward in time (using a snapshot or by dragging the World Time Marker) and assign the next surface to the object. When rendered, Infini-D morphs the three surfaces and a droplet appears and fades away.

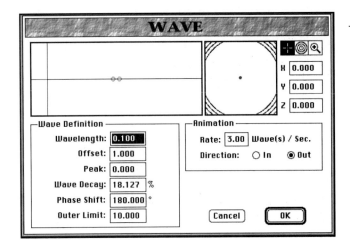

Object Lesson: Clouds and Atmosphere

Setting up an atmosphere successfully can take some tweaking, but the process is fairly simple. It requires ray tracing, but the results are worth the wait. The following steps show you how to construct and animate sky, clouds, and haze.

1. **Begin with a dome.** You can make the dome by placing a sphere and editing it. Delete the bottom part of the rails so that only the top of the sphere remains.

2. **Stretch the dome.** The sky covers a lot of area and our dome needs to as well. Make the X and Y scales very large. The Z scale shouldn't be as large, or it will disappear into the fog, which you will get to in a moment. The width and depth should be at least three to four times the scale of the height.

3. **Create a sky surface.** Choose a sky blue and bring down the specular highlight. That leaves the sky with a flat surface. Turn Glow on 100%. That way the sky won't be affected by lighting differences.

4. **Turn off shadows for the sky dome.** Select the dome and check off the Shadows checkbox in the Object Floater. Now the sky will not cast shadows onto the ground.

5. **Duplicate the sky dome.** Duplicate the sky and align it so that the two domes are exactly on top of each other.

FIGURE 5.100

Good atmospheres take some work.

FIGURE 5.101

A stretched dome forms the sky.

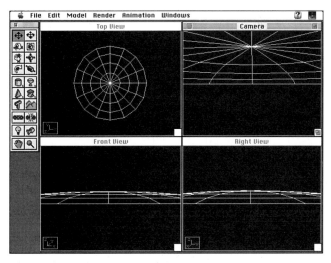

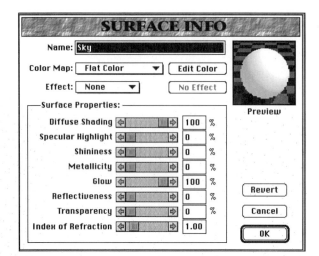

FIGURE 5.102

Plain, flat blue makes a sky surface that won't look like an object just hanging over the scene.

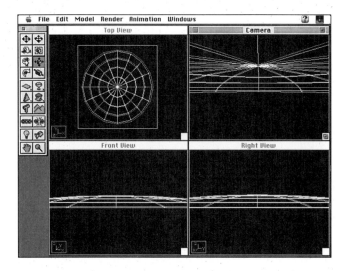

FIGURE 5.103

A second, slightly smaller dome holds the clouds.

6. **Decrease the uniform scale of the new dome.** Make the second dome slightly smaller than the sky. This dome is for the clouds. If you want the clouds to cast shadows on the ground, check Shadows on in the Object Floater.

7. **Create a black and white marble surface.** Marble makes a good cloud cover if adjusted properly. Play with the cohesion and turbulence to get a cloud-like marble. Use white for the clouds and black for the background.

8. **Select the dome and create a composed surface.** Replace white plastic with the marble created in step 7. Turn transparency to 100% and turn off the surface map checkbox.

9. **In the Surface Composition dialog, add a second layer of the marble surface.** Click the Add button and select the same marble surface. Infini-D adds a new layer of the marble. Check the Invert box and turn off Surface. Check Glow on and set it to 100%. This step is necessary to make the clouds bright. By inverting another copy of the surface, the parts that are solid in the transparent layer become the glowing parts in the glow layer.

10. **Scale one of the marble layers down and set infinite repeat.** At the huge scale of the cloud dome, the marble would stretch too much. Because we're using a composed surface, however, we can scale the marble down to a reasonable size. Use the Align With command to make the two marble layers match. The cloud layer is now finished.

FIGURE 5.104

Getting just the right marble can be tricky. A little cohesion, balanced weights, and midrange turbulence usually works well.

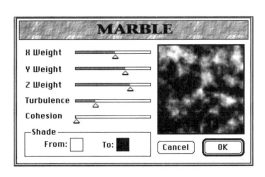

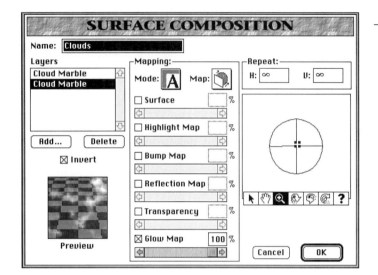

FIGURE **5.105**

Compose a cloud surface using two layers of identical marble, one inverted and glowing and the other a transparency.

11. **Turn on Fog in the Environment dialog.** Set the background color to a light blue, almost white color. The starting point should be very near the viewer and the visibility should be extremely high. The fog now looks like haze, fading to a light bluish-white far off at the horizon.

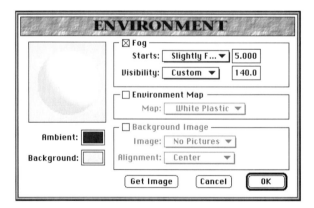

FIGURE **5.106**

Fog takes some tweaking to form haze, especially if the scene is to be animated.

Use a distant light for sunlight, adjusting the color to suit the virtual weather. Add ground terrain, objects, and animation to the scene to complete the world. The clouds can be animated by spinning the cloud dome and by animating the marble. Two or more cloud domes can be used to create layering effects. The more used, though, the more ray tracing slows. Alternatively, the cloud and sky domes can be combined by using a blue and white marble surface. This method limits control and some tricks, such as cloud shadows, are lost. It does, however, elimi-nate the need for ray tracing, and the speed improvements are significant.

At this point, you should be well on your way to creating professional quality surfaces. Of course, there are many things you can do with surfaces, particularly composed surfaces. Explore a little and try new things. If you can imagine a surface, chances are there is a way to create it. In the next chapter, you'll move from sky and clouds to more general environment control and lighting.

Setting the Mood: Environment and Lighting

As any photographer will tell you, environment and lighting are some of the most important aspects of an image. A light in the wrong place or a background that stands out too much detracts from the strength of an image or changes its mood considerably. The same rules that apply to photography apply to both stills and animation in Infini-D. Essentially, Infini-D is creating a photograph of a scene. Thus, the environment and lighting are as important as real-world environment and lighting, even though the scenes might be more fantastic than those in the real world. This chapter demonstrates Infini-D's built-in environmental and lighting controls and helps you build your own environments.

Environment

Infini-D's environmental controls are located in the Environment dialog box (See Figure 6.1). Controls are provided for ambient lighting, background color, background images, environment mapping, and even fog.

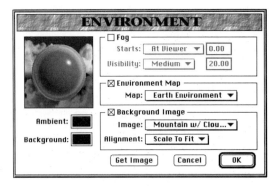

FIGURE 6.1

The Environment dialog

Ambient Lighting

Ambient lighting is one of the most important and, yet, most overlooked environmental controls. Ambient lighting is the fill light that keeps shadows from being pitch black and illuminates the side of your scene facing away from the regular lights.

Click the color box to the right of the word Ambient in the Environment dialog and the Apple Color Picker appears. The color of ambient light controls the hue and the brightness of ambient light. For the most part, just using a white light and altering the brightness is fine. The ambient lighting is not any particular color,

but the brightness affects the darkness of shadows in the scene. Generally, ambient light color should be fairly dark, like the default gray. Real ambient light is actually light reflecting off not-so-reflective objects, so it's not usually very bright.

There are some cases where color is also important. For example, suppose you create an underwater scene. Using a deep aqua-blue for the ambient light color creates dark, but tinted blue shadows. You might use a brighter red-orange color to give a hotter scene some hot-looking ambient light or a faint, cold blue for a room lit with blue neon.

FIGURE 6.2

Ambient light keeps the left side of this object from disappearing into darkness.

FIGURE 6.3

Blue ambient light helps make underwater scenes more watery.

Background Color

The background color of a scene is not quite as important as the ambient lighting, because there are a number of ways to determine the background of a scene. The simplest method, of course, is to choose a background color in the Environment dialog. Alternatively, you can import an image or QuickTime movie to use as a background, or Infini-D can render a scene with an alpha channel and composite it against another background in post-production. Because of the flexibility of a scene's background, the color can be used several different ways. A color can be selected and used as the background of a scene. If the background is an image, or if all of the background is obscured by objects, a color can be selected based on your own preference. The default for Infini-D is black, but you might find it easier or more pleasant to work against a white, gray, or colored background. If, however, you choose to use fog in your scene, be aware that the fog is the same color as the background. Thus, the background color must be the color you want the fog to be.

FIGURE 6.4

Background color is used in this scene as a backdrop.

TIP

Use Force Visible Wireframes with light background colors.

Infini-D is set up to use a black background. As a result, objects with white surfaces or imagemaps are drawn with white wireframes. If you set the background color to a light color, or to white, the objects are invisible. Similarly, if your scene uses a dark background color and dark procedural surfaces, the objects can disappear into the background. If either of these scenarios is the case, choose Window Options from the Windows menu and click the Force Visible Wireframes box. Infini-D now draws all

wireframes in black if the background color is light, or in white if the background color is dark. Repeat the procedure on all windows to make each window draw visible wireframes.

Background Images

The Background Image pop-up menu in the Environment dialog enables you to select PICT or QuickTime movie from the Surface Library to use as a backdrop for your scene. A background image covers the background color, so you are free to select a background color as a working background, rather than as part of your scene. There are a couple of points to note when using background images.

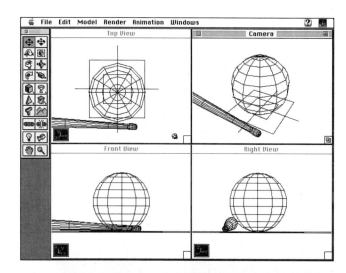

FIGURE 6.5

Force Visible Wireframes makes the wireframes black against light colored backgrounds.

FIGURE 6.6

Background images save the step of compositing against a background image after rendering.

◆ **Objects cannot interact with a background image.** The background is completely independent of all objects in a scene, including the camera. Objects cannot pass through the background, nor cast shadows on it. Infini-D is simply replacing what would normally be a flat background color with an image or animation.

TIP

Texture Map a square to make interactive backgrounds.

Sometimes objects need to interact with the background of a scene, either disappearing into it, casting shadows on it, or even bumping into and shaking it. A background image does not offer this interactivity.

To create an interactive background image, simply apply the image to a square. Orient the square vertically, place it at the back of the scene, and scale the square so that it fills the entire background.

The effect is the same as a standard background image: an image or animation acts as a backdrop for the scene. If the scene needs to be static with respect to camera movement, simply link the square to the camera. The background then moves with the camera, creating the illusion that it is not moving at all.

◆ **Fog and background images don't mix.** Fog and background images conflict on a fundamental level. Fog fades a scene into nothing. A background image is a very well-defined background. Fog can't very well fade into an image or animation, because fog is generally supposed to fade into a thick, opaque background.

◆ **Alpha channels cannot be rendered with a background image.** Because alpha channels composite images and animation onto other backgrounds after rendering, you cannot render an alpha channel when a background image is in use. Alpha channels are essentially a method of telling Infini-D to prepare the rendered images so the background can be inserted later.

Object Lesson: Use Background Images as World Templates

Background images can be used for more than just nice backdrops. You also can use them as templates, or guides, for laying out and animating a scene. For instance, suppose you are creating an animation in which the camera travels through a canyon. The canyon is constructed by applying an imagemap to a terrain. Animation is the tricky part. Here's how to use a template to help set up the animation.

1. **Place the terrain at coordinates (0,0,0).** This is the exact center of the Infini-D World. Placing the terrain here enables us to line it up with the template later.

2. **Import the image used to create the terrain.** The image is already imported for use on the terrain, but it's not yet in the Surface Library. Choose Import Image to load the image into the Surface Library, or click the Get Image button in the Environment dialog.

3. **Turn on Background Image in the Environment dialog.** Click the checkbox next to the Background Image label.

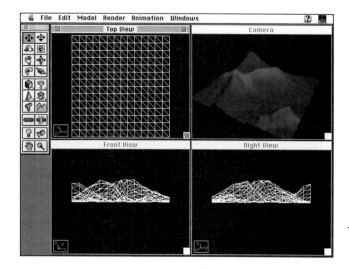

FIGURE 6.7

Without a template, it is difficult to navigate a wireframe terrain in.

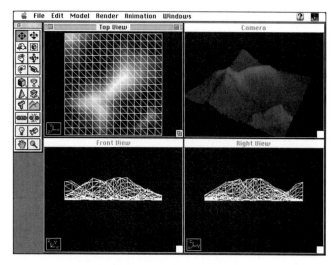

FIGURE 6.8

By using a background image as a template, terrain navigation becomes much easier.

4. **Select the imported image from the Background Image pop-up menu.** The background image now appears in the Camera view when you exit the Background Image dialog.

5. **With the Camera view selected, choose Window Options from the Windows menu.**

6. **Turn *off* Display Background Image.** The background image in the Camera view will not help you, unless you plan to aim the camera down on the terrain from above.

7. **With the Top View selected, choose Window Options from the Windows menu.**

8. **Turn *on* Display Background Image.** The background image now shows up in the Top view.

9. **Use the Uniform Scale tool to match the size of the terrain to the background image.** This step is flexible. You might need to resize the Top view window to display the entire background image. If the background image is set to Scale To Fit, make sure the window is square and not rectangular. Terrains are always square. A rectangular window will distort the background image such that the terrain and background do not line up. Any way you choose to do it, just make sure the terrain and background image line up at the edges.

The background image now acts as a template. The view can be set to wireframe or even bounding box, and you'll still be able to see where the hills and valleys are on the terrain. Animation should be considerably easier.

Environment Maps

Environment maps are a way to fake reflections when ray tracing is not a rendering option. Environment mapping is a much more useful technique, however, than simply as a time-saver. In the real world, surfaces reflect their environment. Metal objects, for example, reflect their environment giving them a shiny, banded look.

FIGURE 6.9

Scenes without environment maps can look flat and unappealing.

FIGURE 6.10

An environment map gives surfaces more life, making them eye-catching and appealing.

It is often too complex and time-consuming to create a complete environment surrounding an object in Infini-D. A single image or animation can be used instead to simulate an environment in a single step. Thus, environment maps are sometimes useful, even when ray tracing is being used. Ray traced surfaces reflect both an environment map and other objects in the scene. The environment map can fill in where the scene itself is not complete.

Here are some tips for creating environment maps.

◆ **Tile images to avoid seams.** Infini-D wraps the environment map around a virtual sphere surrounding the Infini-D World. If the environment map cannot be tiled, a seam forms along the back of the sphere where the edges of the map come together. Sometimes the seam is not noticeable, or the camera is not in a position to see it. Other times, however, the seam can be quite visible. A tiled environment map eliminates the problem altogether.

◆ **Use high-contrast environment maps for metallic surfaces.** Metallic surfaces, such as chrome or gold, need high-contrast environment maps to look good. The reflected effect is a shiny, banded look. The default chrome map in Infini-D is an image of black and white streaks. Metals can be created with environment maps that are not black and white, as long as the colors contrast sharply.

◆ **Use QuickTime movies for animated environments.** Environments are not necessarily static entities. Objects move, light changes, and shadows shift. To simulate active backgrounds, use a QuickTime movie. If possible, the movie should be tiled to avoid seams.

Fog

Fog is an excellent tool for softening or muting backgrounds. Rather than having the farthest edge of a scene be a sharp, visible edge, fog makes the background fade away. Fog can be used to bring the focus of the scene back to the front, to set a misty, foggy mood, or to soften the rear edge of a scene.

FIGURE **6.11**

Mist is just one of fog's many uses.

Infini-D's fog is relatively simple. The farther away from the camera an object is, the more it fades into the background color. As such, the background color determines the color of the fog. A light gray can be used to simulate real fog, light blue for haze, and a dark gray or black to simulate fading into darkness. Getting just the right amount of fog can take a bit of tweaking. Here are some general guidelines for foggy scenes.

◆ **Adjust fog settings based on the scale of your scene.** Fog settings are based on Infini-D World units. Scenes that are built with large scales seem to disappear into the fog much faster than small scenes. This is because the objects are so large that they extend past the visibility limit and disappear. In such a case, use a custom fog setting and make the visibility higher. The presets, low, medium, and high, are relative settings and do not have to be read as low, medium, and high if the scale of the scene does not correspond.

◆ **Real fog starts at the viewer and fades off fairly quickly.** To add realistic fog to a scene, the fog should start at the viewer. Real fog completely surrounds the viewer. The more fog you're looking through, the thicker it seems. The visibility setting depends on how dense you want the fog to look. A medium visibility is usually adequate.

◆ **Haze starts slightly forward and fades off very slowly.** A hazy fog should fade off at the horizon. Haze does not enclose you in a small space the way regular fog does. Starting slightly forward and fading off very slowly to a visibility limit far away makes a hazy fog.

◆ **To soften the back edge of a scene without affecting the rest, start far away.** Fog that starts far away and has a high visibility just softens the back edge. Objects in the foreground are not affected at all.

◆ **Start near the viewer and use low visibility to focus attention on one area.** Much like the single spotlight from above in a dark, smoky room effect, low visibility can enclose a space very tightly. Coupled with a well-placed light or two, such fog can result in some dramatic scenes.

Object Lesson: Animating Fog

Fog, like the rest of the environmental elements, normally cannot be animated. You can animate the rest of the scene, however, and produce an effect like animated fog.

To animate fog, simply link all objects in a scene to the camera. Then, animating the camera uniformly scaling up results in fog rolling in, while animating the camera scaling down results in fog rolling out.

The effect works because child objects are affected by a parent's uniform scale. When the camera scales up, all the children scale up with it. Because the sizes and positions all update relative to each other, the scene does not appear to move. But, because the scale is increasing, the child objects are actually moving farther away from the camera and, thus, disappearing into the fog.

Animating other parts of a scene when all objects are linked to the camera is somewhat tricky, especially if the camera has to move around in the scene. The best thing to do is animate the children moving around the parent camera and leave the camera stationary. That way you won't have to correct for each camera movement when all the children move with the camera.

Lighting

Lighting is even more critical than environmental settings. A single light can have dramatic effects on the mood of a scene. Infini-D has a number of lighting options that enable precise illumination control.

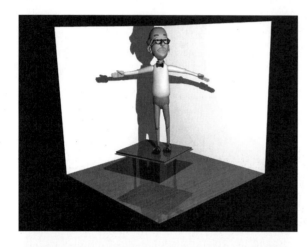

FIGURE 6.12
Point lights cast light in all directions, much like a light bulb.

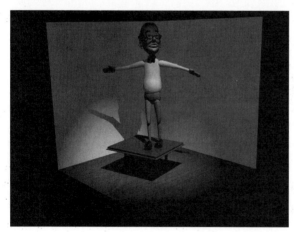

FIGURE 6.13
Spotlights are directional, throwing light only on a specific area.

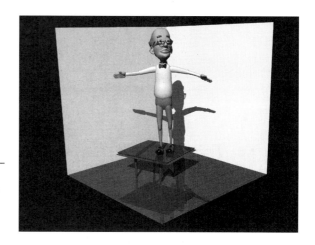

FIGURE 6.14

Distant lights cast light in a direction, but not from any particular point, filling scenes with very even light similar to sunlight.

Aside from ambient lighting, which was discussed in the last section, Infini-D has three light types: point, spot, and distant. Point lights cast light in all directions from a single point, much like a lightbulb. Spotlights also cast light from a single point, but the light is directional, much like a flashlight. Distant lights cast directional light, but not from any particular point. As a result, the light rays are parallel instead of spreading out like a spotlight. The effect is light similar to sunlight where the source is so far away that the light casts evenly.

Each light type has an interactive preview window associated with it in the Light Floater. The Point Light preview has two rings encircling a lightbulb. These two rings represent the beginning and end of the *light falloff*. In other words, the inner ring marks where the light begins to fade and the outer ring marks where the light fade ends. Manipulating the light falloff can change a light significantly. Candlelight, for example, starts to fade quickly and doesn't fade for very long. A 100-watt lightbulb, on the other hand, casts fairly far before starting to fade visibly, and then has a long, soft fade.

FIGURE 6.15

The Point Light floater offers light falloff, color, and intensity control.

FIGURE **6.16**

Spotlights have cone angle, falloff, and other controls similar to point lights.

Spotlights also have falloff values. A spotlight's falloff values are represented in the preview by two curves on the right side of the Preview Box. Spotlights have another set of lines in the preview, as well. These lines set the cone of the spotlight and act as a light cone falloff. The inner pair of lines is the fully illuminated cone, and the outer pair is the edge of the falloff. Think of the cone settings as a spotlight focus of sorts. The wider the cone, the wider the area of light cast by the spotlight. Narrow the cone to concentrate the spotlight on a smaller area.

Distant lights do not have falloff or cone settings, because the light is uniform and parallel. Consequently, the interactive preview is quite different. Because distant lights have no position, the preview contains a tool that is similar to the virtual trackball in the modeler. This tool sets the direction of the light. Click the small white disk representing the light and drag to rotate it. The line extending from the disk represents the direction of the light. The trackball has full rotational control of the light, so you can set the light to any angle.

All of Infini-D's light types can be edited numerically. Double-click the light or click the Light Info button on the Light Floater. A dialog appears that enables you to set precise falloff values, cone angles, directions, and other options. Additionally, the Light Info dialog enables you to enter values that are larger than the interactive previews normally permit. Light falloff, for example, has a limit of 100 in the preview window. In the Light Info dialog, however, the falloff value can be set much higher than 100, making lights that cast much farther than otherwise possible.

FIGURE **6.17**

Distant lights do not have falloff values, but do have a unique direction control.

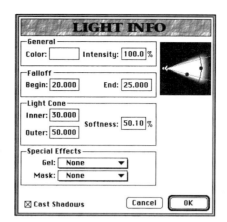

FIGURE 6.18

The Light Info dialog lets you select surfaces, images, or QuickTime movies to use as gels and masks on your spotlights.

Masks and Gels

Two pop-up menus appear in the Light Info dialog for spotlights that are not found in other Light Info dialogs. These menus are for selecting *gels* and *masks*. Both menus enable you to select any surface, image, or QuickTime movie to apply to the spotlight. While any light can have a color applied by clicking the color box in the light floater, a gel can be multicolored, a specific image, or even an animated QuickTime movie. A gel uses the surface's color information to cast light of the same color.

Masks use the grayscale, or brightness, information of a surface, image, or QuickTime movie to block light. To create the effect of light shining through a window, use Photoshop to create a PICT image in which a black window frame surrounds white windowpanes. When applied to a spotlight, light cast through the panes of the window leave shadows as if the light were shining through a real window. A mask as simple as a window frame can add immeasurable realism to a scene. Masks and gels can be used together to add even more to a scene.

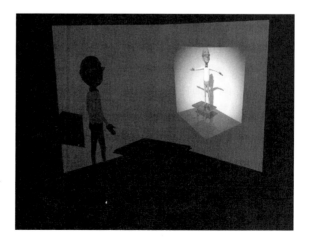

FIGURE 6.19

Among myriad other uses, a gel can project an image or animation onto a wall like a slide or movie projector.

FIGURE **6.20**
*Sun shining through trees can be
simulated using a mask.*

There is only one catch to gels and masks. A scene must be rendered in Shade-Best or Ray Trace, because the gel or mask is a procedural surface or an image. As a result, a rendering mode that supports procedural surfaces or imagemaps is necessary. Fast or Better shading is affected by gels and masks, but the results are generally blurry, indistinguishable changes in color. Best shading loads the surfaces properly and gives stunning results.

Padding a Mask

When a mask is applied to a spotlight, the image covers the entire area of light. Because spotlights naturally cast circular light patterns, the corners of a mask are clipped. To avoid this clipping, *pad out* the edges of the image by adding a black border. The black border will block any light and appear invisible. At the same time, the white parts of the mask are forced onto the visible part of the light instead of being clipped. The end result is that an irregularly shaped mask can remain irregularly shaped, instead of being cut into a circle.

TIP

To increase the image size of a square image minimally, simply increase the size by *141 percent*. That magic number increases the size just enough so that the corners of the mask are not cut. If the image is not square, increase the largest side by 141 percent, and then make the shorter side the same size.

Negative Light

Point, spot, and distant lights all have an intensity value. By default, this value is 100. Increasing the value makes very bright lights and decreasing it makes dim lights. The intensity of a light, however, is not limited to positive numbers. Try entering a negative value and watch what happens to objects around the light. A *negative light* seems to pull light out of a scene, thereby casting a pool of shadow instead of a pool of light. The more negative a light is, the more light it absorbs from a scene.

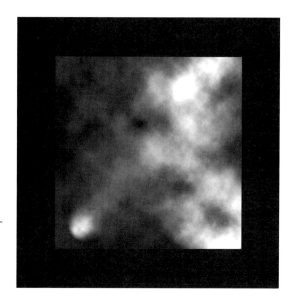

FIGURE 6.21

A square or irregularly shaped mask can have its shape preserved by adding black padding to the edges of the image.

FIGURE 6.22

Negative light has interesting effects when rendered with shadows, casting pools of shadow and shadows of light.

Negative lights also can be colored, just as a normal light. But where a normal red light, for example, casts red, a negative red light pulls red out, leaving other colors behind. Masks and gels work with negative lights as well, but the effects are reversed. A negative light mask casts shadow through the white parts of the mask and shines light through the black.

Summary

Lighting can make or break a scene. Just as a candlelight dinner isn't very romantic if fluorescent lights are left on, an Infini-D scene won't have the right mood without the right lighting. It's worth the time (if you can spare it) to keep playing with the lights until the scene is exactly right. Gels and masks make scene setting much easier. Anyone involved with lighting theatrical productions can attest to the importance of gels and masks (or *gobos*, as they are called in theatre).

Now, in addition to Infini-D basics, working efficiently, and building and surfacing models, you've learned something about creating a world for the models. You now know how to build a scene from start to finish, with the exception of animating it. The next couple of chapters delve into some slightly more specific topics. If 3D text and flying logos are your mission, the next chapter shows you what to do.

3D Text & Logos

A very powerful aspect of Infini-D is its capability to create a logo or block of 3D text that appears to be carved from a chunk of chrome or gold. You've doubtless seen this effect on television before a football game or in a movie where metal text flies around your screen.

To create these *flying logo* effects, you need to use a technique known as an *environment map*. An environment map is a PICT file that Infini-D reflects off the surface of a logo or 3D text. If you use an environment map with contrasting blacks and whites, you'll get the appearance of highlights, which creates the metallic effect for which the flying logos are famous.

Creating and Loading an Environment Map

1. **Choose Import from the File menu.** In the Import submenu, choose the Image option. Select a PICT file to use as an environment map.

2. **Choose the Environment... option under the Render menu.**

3. **In the Environment dialog box, click the checkbox for Environment Map and choose the PICT you imported from the pop-up list.** The PICT that you imported is located at the bottom of the list.

Here is another method for creating an environment map in Infini-D 3.1.

1. **Using the Finder, locate the environment map you want and drag-and-drop it into your Infini-D World window.** It becomes a background picture.

2. **In the Environment dialog, uncheck Background Image.**

Check Environment Map and choose the texture you dragged into the window.

Remember, the colors in the environment map blend with the colors of the surface of your logo (plus the ambient lighting). Here are some examples:

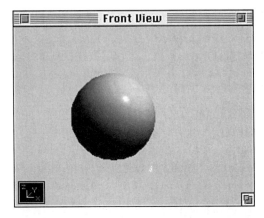

FIGURE **7.1**
White Plastic Surface

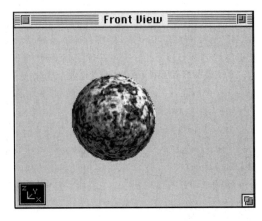

FIGURE **7.2**
Polished Marble Surface

FIGURE 7.3

PICT image of Hayden logo

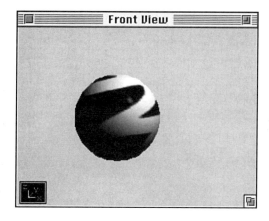

FIGURE 7.4

Environment map of Hayden logo

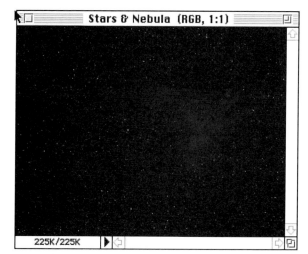

FIGURE 7.5

PICT image of stars

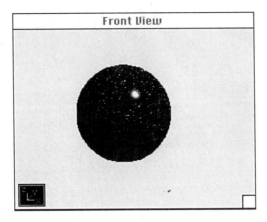

FIGURE 7.6

Environment map of stars

Create Your Own Environment Map with Photoshop

1. Choose New from the File menu, 256×256 image, grayscale.

2. Fill the background with black.

3. Choose a soft brush and paint some white streaks.

4. Choose Noise from the Filter menu, setting 50.

5. Choose Motion Blur from the Filter menu, radial, distance 3 pixels.

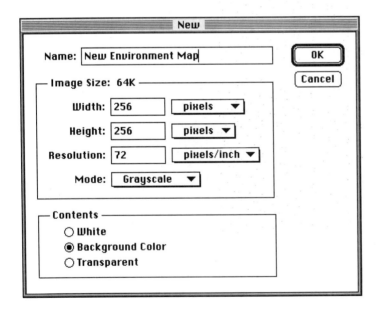

FIGURE 7.7

New dialog box

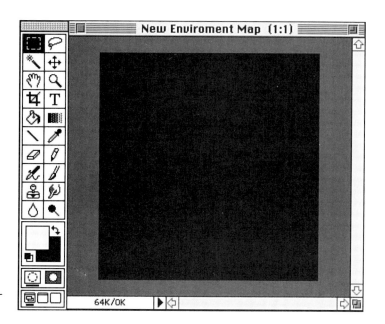

FIGURE 7.8
Black background

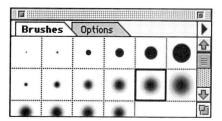

FIGURE 7.9
Brushes

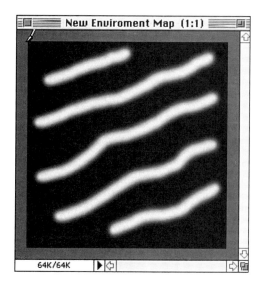

FIGURE 7.10
Paint some white streaks.

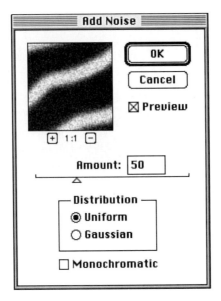

FIGURE 7.11
Add Noise dialog box

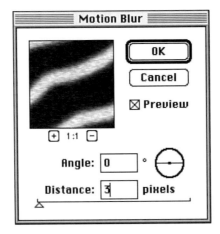

FIGURE 7.12
Motion Blur dialog box

FIGURE 7.13

New environment map

Create Your Own Environment Map with Infini-D

If you don't own a paint program, you can make your own environment maps with Infini-D.

1. **In the Render menu, choose New Surface.**

2. **In the Surface Info dialog box, choose Noise from the Color Map pop-up menu.** Click the Edit Color box. The

Shade box of the Noise dialog that appears enables you to adjust the color variation of the surface. Use the Density slider to set the density at about 50 percent. See Figure 7.17. Clicking the From and To boxes brings up the Apple Color Picker dialog. Make the color range from black to white.

FIGURE 7.14

New Surface command

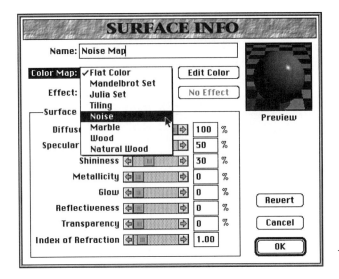

FIGURE 7.15
Surface Info dialog box

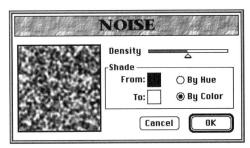

FIGURE 7.16
Noise dialog box

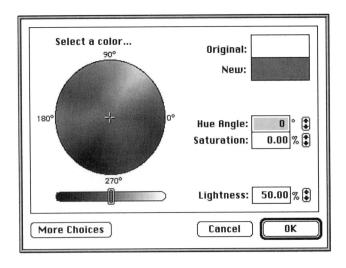

FIGURE 7.17
Apple Color Picker

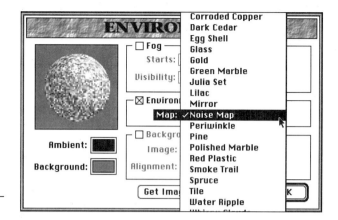

FIGURE 7.18

Environment dialog box

3. **At the top of the New Surface dialog box, give your surface map a unique name.**

4. **Open the Environment dialog box, click Environment Map, and choose the surface you just created.**

You have created a procedural environment map! The good news is that this takes less RAM than a PICT-based environment map. The bad news is that your scene takes longer to render.

EPS Images

EPS images cannot be imported into Infini-D. Path outlines must be created around the image. It is *very* common for people to scan a logo, save it as an EPS image in Photoshop, and then try to open it in Infini-D.

Before the logo can be imported into Infini-D, it must be traced with paths. You can do this manually using the Photoshop Path tools (Pen tool) or you can use the Magic Wand tool. The Path tools offer a more accurate alternative, and

are located in the Paths palette under the Window menu. Use these tools to trace your logo.

If you use the Magic Wand tool, select the entire logo using the tool and the Shift key. When the logo is selected, and everything else is deselected, choose Make Paths in the Paths Palette menu. Save the path by choosing Export from the File menu and Paths to Illustrator from the Export submenu.

In Infini-D, choose Import EPS... from the File menu.

For more information on Adobe Photoshop, I recommend *Adobe Photoshop Classroom in a Book*, published by Adobe Press (see Appendix C).

TIP

Photoshop LE does not have Path tools and cannot convert scanned images to path outlines. Adobe Streamline is a program specifically designed to convert images to path outlines. Read more about Streamline at `http://www.adobe.com/Apps/ Streamline.html`.

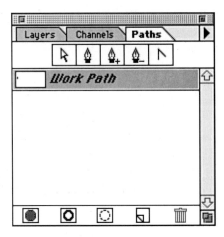

FIGURE 7.19

Paths Palette in Photoshop

Object Lesson: Creating a Framed Logo

Another cool effect is to have a logo perfectly framed within a 3D rectangle. To do this:

1. **Import an EPS version of your logo.** Choose EPS… from the Import submenu under the File menu.

2. **Double-click your logo, or choose Edit Object from the Model menu.**

3. **Choose the Rectangle tool.**

4. **Hold down the ⌘ key and click where you want the outside of the rectangle to be.** Holding down the ⌘ key forces the Rectangle tool to draw from the center of your object.

FIGURE 7.20

Rectangle tool

Make sure that the path is closed, unless you want a thin, extruded logo. Also, text created in Illustrator needs to be made into paths. From the Type menu, choose Make Outlines. Text is automatically translated into path outlines.

Now your logo should look something like this.

If you want to create a double framed logo, simply repeat the procedure, placing a second rectangle outside the first. The distance between the two rectangles defines a border for your object.

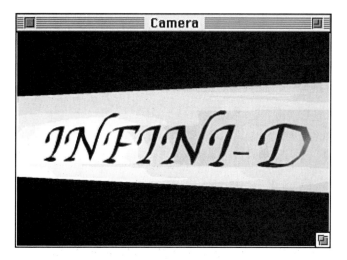

FIGURE 7.21
Framed logo

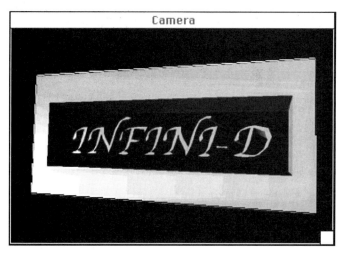

FIGURE 7.22
Double framed logo

FIGURE 7.23
Circle tool

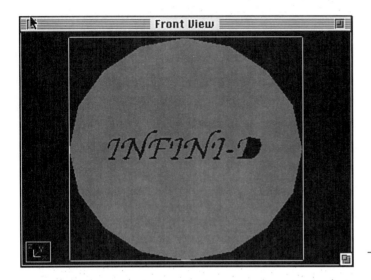

FIGURE 7.24
Circle logo

This technique works equally well with the Circle tool. When drawing the circle, depending on the shape of your logo, you may want to hold down the Shift key while holding the ⌘ key and drawing your circle. This assures that you have a perfect circle around your object.

Compositing a Logo Against a Background in Photoshop

If you want to composite your logo against a Photoshop background, use the following steps. This is a useful technique for product previews and visualization.

1. **Create your logo and position it as desired in the Camera window.**

2. **Choose Window Options from the Window menu.**

3. **Choose Millions for the color depth and Straight for the Alpha Channel.**

4. **Render your logo with the desired rendering and anti-aliasing quality.**

5. **Save your image as a PICT file.**

6. **Open your PICT in Photoshop. Choose Load Selection from the Select menu and Click OK.**

7. **Choose Copy from the Edit menu.**

8. **Open your background, and choose Paste from the Edit menu.**

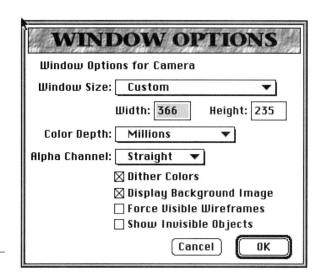

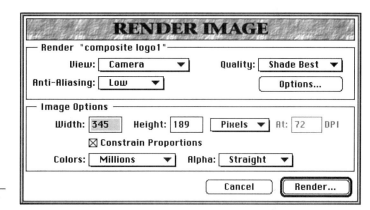

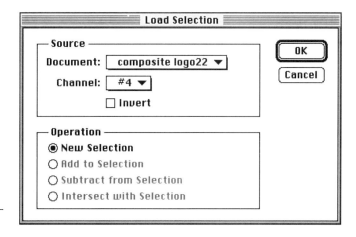

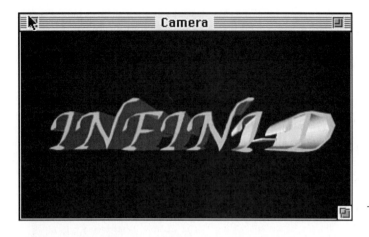

FIGURE 7.28
Logo

FIGURE 7.29
Photoshop background

Photoshop seamlessly composites your Infini-D logo against the background. Note that the quality of the alpha channel corresponds directly to the level of anti-aliasing you selected.

You can reproduce this technique at high-resolutions via Infini-D's Render Image dialog, located under the File menu in the Render submenu's Image… option. If you want to render your image at a specific resolution, choose Inches for the measurement component and type in the desired resolution.

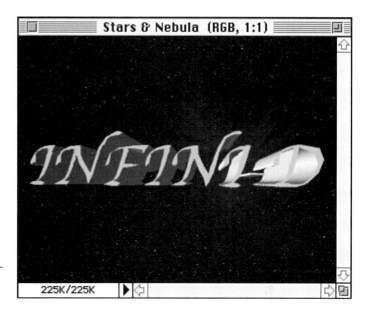

FIGURE 7.30

Logo successfully composited into Photoshop image

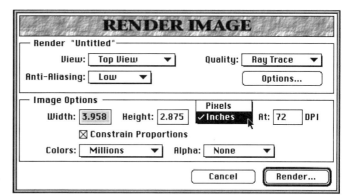

FIGURE 7.31

Render Image dialog box

Compositing a Logo Against a Background in Premiere

You can also composite text or a 3D logo using this same technique in products such as Adobe Premiere or Avid Videoshop. In this case, Premiere or Videoshop composites the text over a still background or a video in the same way that Adobe Photoshop would. It's the equivalent of choosing Photoshop's Load Selection, Copy, and Paste for each frame of the movie.

Say, for example, you want to fly through the text of your logo, and then composite this against a Premiere background.

Infini-D

1. **Set up your animation. Press ⌘+M or choose Snapshot from the Animation menu.** Select the Uniform Scale tool (third down from the top on the right side of the Toolbox) and increase the size of your logo. This is easier than manipulating the camera and provides the same effect.

For more information see Chapter 10, "Animation."

2. **Choose Render from the File menu.** Choose Animation... in the Render submenu.

3. **Set up your animation parameters. Select a Straight alpha channel. Click Render.**

4. **Export as the files as QuickTime.** Click on Options in the Output dialog box, choose Animation as the compressor, and choose Millions+ as your color depth.

Premiere

1. **Load your Infini-D QuickTime Movie and your background.**

2. **Put the background in the A or B track and the movie in the S1 track.**

3. **Select your movie and choose Transparency from Clip menu (⌘+T).**

4. **Choose Alpha Channel for the transparency option.**

Now, when you render or preview your Premiere movie, it seamlessly composites every frame of your Infini-D animation over the background.

This is not a Premiere book, but these are such great tips I included them anyway.

Tip #1: Use the Rubber Band option in your QuickTime clip (it appears after you select the alpha channel transparency) to make your Infini-D 3D element fade in and out. It works especially well with a cloud texture.

Tip #2: Use the Pan Image filter on your background. Select the background and choose Filter from the Image menu (⌘+F). This moves the background underneath your 3D animation—a great effect!

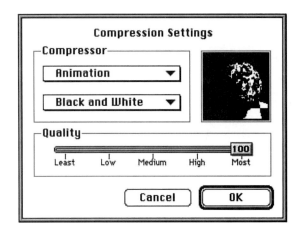

FIGURE 7.32
Compression Settings

Coming at ya! Text Effects

1. **Place your text in the Infini-D World.**

2. **Open your Object Floater (Windows menu, Object Floater).**

3. **Type 0,0,0 in the X, Y, and Z position to center your object.**

4. **In the Views floater, select Front Default from the Bookmarks pop-up menu (Camera window must also be selected).**

5. **Select the Squash & Stretch tool (fourth down on the right side of the Toolbox) and move your mouse up. This zooms the text zoom out toward you.**

6. **Choose the Rotate Towards/Away tool (second from the top on the left side of the Toolbox) and rotate the text upward (move the mouse up).**

> **TIP**
>
> Double-click Rotate tools to set *snap angles*. In this case, a snap angle of 15 degrees puts the text in the perfect position.

Fisheye Lens Effect

Select the camera (or choose Camera from the Select option beneath the Model menu) and choose Edit Camera in the Model menu (or just double-click the camera). Select Fisheye under the Lens Type pop-up and place the camera very close to your text object. This will amplify the "coming at ya" effect in interesting ways...

FIGURE 7.33

Now the text is "Coming at ya!"

FIGURE 7.34

Fisheye lens effect

Curvy Text

To make curvy text (say to wrap it around a 3D sphere):

1. **Select the Text tool and type `Curvy Text` into the Text dialog.**

2. **Choose Break into characters from the Model menu.** This breaks the text into individual, editable objects with each character linked to the first letter of your text.

> **NOTE**
>
> Make sure that you position and size your text as a whole before you break it into its composite characters. You cannot Undo after you break the text into characters.

3. **Choose the Unlink tool (looks like a broken chain) and click each letter in the Front view.**

4. **Relink the characters. Start with the last character and work backward to the first, forming a chain.**

5. **Select the second character and change the Y rotate component to 20 degrees. Press Return. Repeat this step for each character.**

> **TIP**
>
> Use the Sequencer for linking and unlinking. Simply drag the object you want to link onto the object to which you want to link it. You can also unlink objects in the Sequencer by dragging them between objects.

FIGURE 7.35

Object floater Y value

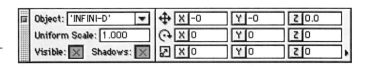

FIGURE 7.36

Curvy Text

FIGURE 7.37

Curvy Text

You can experiment with the curves by making the Y rotational factor larger or smaller. Try experimenting with the X and Z rotational factors as well.

The *Circularity Animation Assistant*, written by David Hirmes, can streamline some of these effects. However, understanding the underlying principle enables you to apply this technique to other objects such as chains or cords.

Also, try using this technique over time. You can animate a normal, flat piece of text into a curvy piece of text with great effect. For example, you can have a piece of text unfurling like a rug or blowing in the wind like a flag.

Beveled Text

A bevel consists of typeface lines that do not meet at right angles. These can be applied to text created in the Infini-D World.

Bevels, including Back Bevel, mean more polygons and longer rendering times, but can create some nice text effects.

1. Click the Text tool in the Toolbar.

2. Click in the Infini-D World where you want to place the Text. A dialog box appears.

3. In the Text dialog, select a font. Click the button labeled Bevel.

4. Select the bevel you want to use, and make sure that Back Bevel remains unchecked unless you want a back bevel.

5. At the left side of the dialog is the Bevel Editor. Click and drag to create a custom bevel.

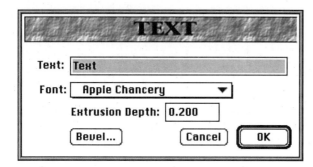

FIGURE 7.38
Text dialog box

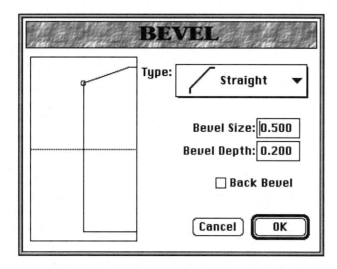

FIGURE 7.39
Bevel dialog box

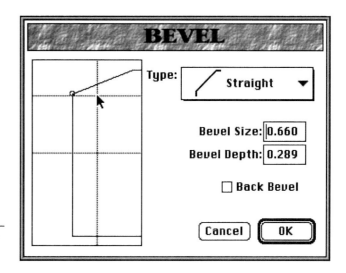

FIGURE 7.40

Creating a custom bevel with the Bevel Editor.

Chiseled Text

A popular effect is to have a logo appear as though it was carved out of solid steel. To accomplish this, you give the frame of the logo a chiseled effect.

1. **Choose Import EPS... from the File menu.**

Absynthe Power Tools

Absynthe Power Tools, written by Chris Bernardi, is a collection of incredibly powerful techniques for Infini-D.

These tools, created by Absynthe, an Idaho-based graphics and animation shop, are available at Specular's Web site:

```
http://www.specular.com/support/tips/
apt/apt.html
```

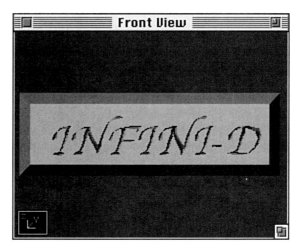

FIGURE 7.41

Chiseled text

However, there are newer ways to deal with surface bevels.

Beveling Text with Different Surfaces—Decal Mode

Putting a different surface on the front, sides, and bevel of a text object or logo is an excellent effect that makes text really stand out. Edges can be made to glow, shine, or reflect. The front and sides can appear to be made of different materials. You can even make the bevels transparent. Here's how to make stone text with chrome sides and an elegant gold bevel.

1. **Create a text object or logo and apply a bevel.** Any size or shape bevel will do. Just be sure it's large enough to be visible. A flat bevel is perfect for making gold bevels.

2. **With the object still selected, choose Compose Surface from the Render menu.**

3. **Replace the White Plastic layer with an image or procedural surface.**

This is the surface for the front face of the object. It can be either an image or a procedural, because it is the bottom layer. Green Marble gives the front of the text a stone look. Leave the surface in Straight Map mode; it needs to lie flat on the front and back faces of the text. Ignore the sides for now.

4. **Add a layer and load a black image.** The sides and bevel are reflective and a black layer provides that reflectivity. Turn off the surface attribute and adjust the reflectiveness to 70%. Switch the Mapping Mode to Decal. The black layer is then applied only to the sides of the object (decals cannot be applied to end caps).

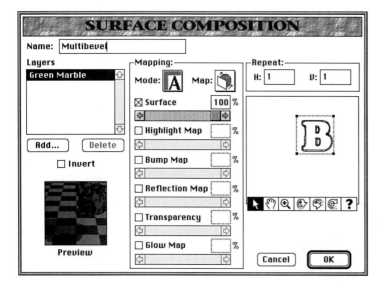

FIGURE 7.43

Reflections are controlled by a black image layer applied to the sides and bevel of the text.

5. **Add a layer and load a gold image.** The bevel surface comes next. Set the Mapping Mode to Decal again and leave everything else alone. Combined with the black layer, the sides of the object, including bevels, should be gold.

6. **Add a layer and load a chrome image.** The chrome image should just be a gray square. As with the gold layer, the black takes care of reflections. Switch the Mapping Mode to Decal and rotate the object so the sides and bevels are visible. Pull the V slider's handles in so that the red lines denoting the top and bottom of the chrome layer come just to the edge of the bevel, but do not extend over the bevel. The chrome will then cover only the sides of the object, letting the gold show through on the bevels.

7. **Exit the Compose Surface dialog and load a chrome environment map.** Render in Shade Best or Ray Trace.

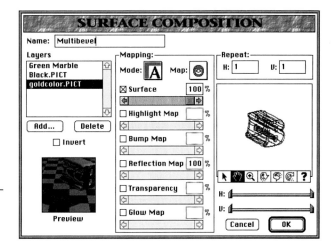

FIGURE 7.44

Apply a gold layer over the black to cover the sides and bevel with gold trim.

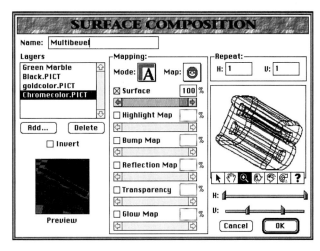

FIGURE 7.45

Finally, a chrome layer applied to the sides leaves gold bevels and a stone face.

2.24M

Figure 7.46

The final rendered text has a stone front, gold trim bevels, and chrome sides.

Summary

One of the most powerful aspects of Infini-D is its capability to create a logo or block of 3D text that appears to be carved from a chunk of chrome of gold. Now that you have a basic knowledge of how Infini-D works with text, experiment with your own ideas for logos, decals, and composited text. The possibilities are infinite.

Terrains

Building an indoor scene, with a floor, ceiling, and four walls, is fairly simple. A few squares lined up on their edges with appropriate surfaces are quite passable as a room's interior. Only a handful of scenes, however, take place in a setting as simple as a square room. Many outdoor scenes, such as a mountain, riverbed, or the surface of the moon, need rough, irregular landscapes. Such settings are too difficult to construct even using the Workshop. Infini-D's Terrain tool is the solution.

Modeling Mountains: Using Terrains in Infini-D

A terrain is a flat square very similar to the squares used to create the room, but, whereas a square is limited to single, flat polygons, terrains consist of many smaller polygons that do not have to remain flat. Infini-D provides a number of mathematically defined shapes for terrains. Different shapes can be defined through the use of a grayscale terrain map, accessible via Image in the Terrain Type pop-up menu.

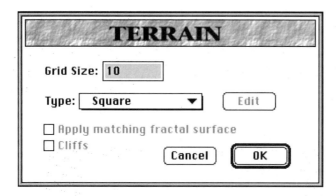

FIGURE 8.1

Terrains are customizable through the Terrain dialog.

Though the mathematically defined terrains are useful, they are limited. The two fractal terrains and the noise terrain are the only customizable built-in terrains, but are limited to a single fractal or Infini-D's standard noise. The real power of terrains is the use of image terrains. An image terrain uses an image, or terrain map, to raise and lower the terrain's polygons.

Terrain Maps

Terrain maps function like bump maps for a terrain. Any grayscale PICT image can be used. Black areas are sunken in the terrain and white areas are raised. Grays are in between. Creating a successful terrain map, using a paint program such as Adobe Photoshop or Fractal Painter, is the trickiest part of image terrain building. It takes some experimentation and practice to get just what you want. Here are the steps to building a mountain in Photoshop.

1. **Create a new image.** A terrain is always square, so, to prevent distortion of your terrain map, the image should be square also. The size can vary depending on the necessary detail and the available disk space. For now, use 300 pixels by 300

pixels. Set the mode to grayscale and the background to black.

2. **Use the Gradient tool to put a circle in the middle of the image.** The gradient should go from white to transparent (that way you can layer multiple circles if you want) and should be set to radial to create a circle instead of a straight gradient.

3. **Use the Add Noise option from the Noise submenu under Filter to roughen the surface.** Don't add too much noise. A little will do.

4. **Blur the noise with the Radial Blur option found in the Blur submenu beneath the Filter menu.** Set the Radial Blur filter to Zoom instead of Spin, and set the blur to 15. The noise streaks down the side of the mountain.

5. **Apply the Wave filter found in the Distort submenu beneath the Filter menu.** The mountain needs a random shape; the regular radial gradient will create a cone. Applying Wave distorts the gradient very nicely. You can tweak the settings until you get a shape you like, or you can hit the Randomize button until you see something good.

FIGURE 8.2

Start with a radial gradient from white to a black background.

FIGURE 8.3

Noise roughens the surface of the terrain.

FIGURE 8.4

Blur the noise into streaks running out from the center.

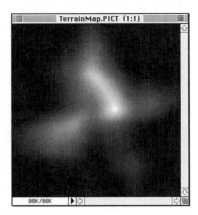

FIGURE 8.5

Use the Wave filter to make a more natural shape.

6. Blur the peaks of the mountain with the Gaussian Blur option found in the Blur submenu beneath the Filter menu. Use the Lasso to encircle the peaks of the mountain, the lightest parts of the image. In the Feather dialog box, found under the Select menu, set the selection to 10 pixels and apply a slight Gaussian Blur. This smoothes out the top of the mountain where the surface would be worn the most. You might want to brighten the peak slightly after the Gaussian Blur by using the Brightness/Contrast command found in the Adjust submenu of the Image menu.

7. Save the image as a PICT file.

TIP

DEMView, written by Ken Badertscher, is a utility that turns USGS Digital Elevation Model data into grayscale images perfect for building terrains in Infini-D. The program is free and topographical information is available on the Internet. If you've ever wanted to model a real piece of land, or if you just need an extremely realistic terrain, DEMView is the tool you need. Find it at `ftp://emr1.emr.ca/gsc/hbrand/`.

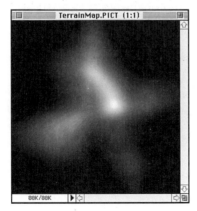

FIGURE 8.6

Soften and smooth the top of the mountain by blurring the whitest parts.

You're now ready to build a mountain. In Infini-D, place a terrain and double-click it to edit it, or press ⌘+E. Now, in the Terrain dialog box, select Image from the bottom of the type list pop-up menu. Click the Edit button to select and load an image.

The grid size determines the detail of the terrain. The higher the grid size, the more polygons the terrain will have. Of course, the more polygons, the slower it is. For this reason, the best way to work with terrains is at a low grid size and with the aid of a background image template (see Chapter 6, "Environment and Lighting," for instructions on using an image as a template). Then, for test rendering, set the grid size higher, say to 50. For final rendering, you might want to set the grid size even higher to get the maximum detail out of the terrain.

Back in the Infini-D World, the terrain takes on the shape defined by the terrain map. Open the Object floater and set the Z dimension to 0.500. A setting of 1.000 is generally too high to look realistic. Use the Uniform Scale setting to reduce or enlarge the entire terrain.

Terrain Surfaces

The most detailed terrain map won't look very good with a shiny white plastic surface. A terrain map needs a surface map as well. The easiest way to get a matching surface map is to colorize your terrain map. Open it in Photoshop, set the mode to RGB, and start painting. You can use a soft brush or airbrush to hand paint colors and gradients onto the mountain, or you can use filtering and color adjustments to create a surface that exactly matches the mountain. Be sure to Save As when you're finished, so that you don't save over your terrain map.

The roughness of the terrain surface cannot compare to the detail of a bump map. Again, use the terrain map, add a little more noise, and perhaps increase the contrast slightly. Save with a different name, so that you don't wipe out your terrain map.

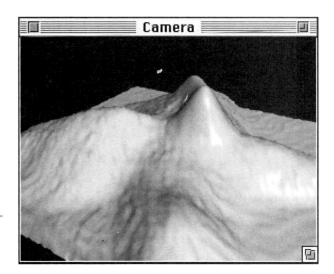

FIGURE 8.7

The terrain map is applied to a terrain to create a landscape for a scene.

FIGURE 8.8

The terrain map can be used to make matching surfaces and bump maps.

TIP

Quite often, the terrain map is detailed enough to serve also as the bump map. You'll have to load it a second time (because loading as a terrain image will not load the image as a surface), and then apply the image as a bump map in a composed surface.

When you're finished making surfaces in Photoshop, switch back to Infini-D. Select the terrain and choose Compose Surface from the Render menu. Add a layer and load the surface map. Add a second layer and load the bump map. The bump map should have the surface attribute checked off and the bump attribute checked on. The bump amount can be adjusted via the bump slider, but the default of 50% is usually a good size. If the bump is set too high, it will be too pronounced. If it is set it too low, it won't be visible.

Experiment with different ways to build the terrain maps. A specific shape can be designed by hand painting with a soft brush in Photoshop, or custom gradients can be designed with Kai's Power Tools. More or less noise, different blurs, or custom smudging are all ways to fine-tune a terrain map. Try setting the background color to 50% gray. That way you can have both mountains, by painting with white and lighter grays, and valleys, gorges, or canyons, by painting with black and darker grays.

TIP

The size of a terrain map's gradient determines the steepness of the hills and valleys in the terrain. A wide, slow gradient creates smooth, gentle slopes. A narrower gradient that fades very quickly defines cliffs. To mix and match gentle hills and steep cliffs, use feathered selections and blurring to blend gradients together.

Terrains don't have to be used for landscapes. The water in figure 8.10 was made with a terrain and bump map. Less organic gradients can be used to build different sorts of sets. Graduated steps, for example, create stairs. Unfortunately, terrains cannot be animated, so liquid terrains are better suited to still shots.

Building terrains is the last modeling option in Infini-D. The next chapter shows you how to use other modelers in conjunction with Infini-D, so that you can take advantage of the best of many modeling worlds.

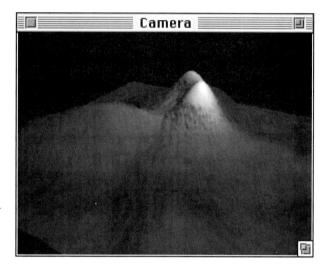

FIGURE **8.9**

Bump and surface maps applied to the terrain give it a much more realistic appearance.

FIGURE **8.10**

Terrains are not limited to land forms. The water in this scene is a terrain with a bump map.

Importing 3D Objects

Every modeler has its limitations. One modeler might be good at building organic objects, while another might specialize in CAD-accurate design. Some modelers sport advanced features like Constructive Solid Geometry (often referred to as Boolean functions). Others can distort and warp objects from the whole down to individual polygons. Infini-D's Workshop is a modeler with strengths and weaknesses just like any other modeler.

Fortunately, you are not limited to using a single software package as your only modeler. You can take advantage of the strengths of almost any modeler available to build exactly the objects you need. Switching modeling environments is possible because of common file formats, such as DXF and 3DMF. Many different software packages can read and write these formats, enabling you to move object files between environments. Thus, modeling can be done in one environment, while animation and rendering are done in another.

FIGURE 9.1

Infini-D 3.1 does not have the capability to cut parts out of an object. A separate modeler must be used to create the objects and save them in a format Infini-D can read.

Infini-D imports three different file formats: DXF, 3DMF, and Swivel. The first two are popular formats. The third is not particularly common and is only used in conjunction with Swivel 3D Pro.

DXF is the most common format. DXF was developed by AutoDesk for AutoCAD and 3D Studio. Cross-platform compatibility and the popularity of AutoDesk's products make DXF a widely used format. Unfortunately, DXF is also a very loose format. That is, each product that reads and writes DXF does so in its own way and not always with predictable results. The surface information stored in a DXF is limited, and the size of files can be rather large due to the text format used to store model information. Still, DXF can describe almost any model, so anything you build can be represented in a DXF.

3DMF is a relatively new format developed by Apple Computer as part of QuickDraw 3D. 3DMF has eliminated many of the problems associated with DXF. Most notably, reading and writing files is done at the system level, meaning that files are more compatible. Also, system level integration creates more intuitive, natural import and export options, such as drag-and-drop.

Importing DXF

DXF files can be imported into Infini-D via the Import Objects option in the File menu. A File Open dialog appears with a pop-up menu at the bottom. Select DXF from the pop-up menu and locate the DXF file on your hard drive. Click Open. Infini-D displays a DXF import options dialog (see Figure 9.3).

FIGURE **9.2**

The DXF Import dialog starts with fewer choices by default.

```
┌─────────────────────────────────────────────┐
│  ┌───────────────────────────────────────┐  │
│  │        Options for DHF™ Import         │  │
│  │                                        │  │
│  │  Smooth Edges:                         │  │
│  │       ○ Always                         │  │
│  │       ○ Never                          │  │
│  │       ◉ Smoothing Angle:  │ 90 │ °     │  │
│  │                                        │  │
│  │  ☒ Scale And Center    ☒ Link Objects  │  │
│  │  ☐ One Object Per Layer ☒ Use Color Info│ │
│  │                                        │  │
│  │ ┌────────────┐  ┌────────┐ ┌────────┐  │  │
│  │ │Fewer Choices│  │ Cancel │ │   OK   │  │  │
│  │ └────────────┘  └────────┘ └────────┘  │  │
│  └───────────────────────────────────────┘  │
└─────────────────────────────────────────────┘
```

FIGURE 9.3

Click the More Choices button. A DXF import dialog with additional import options appears.

The dialog at first is very simple. Three smoothing choices are presented. These options enable the user to select how Infini-D smoothes the edges of polygons. Click the More Choices option and a new dialog with more control over the import process appears (see Figure 9.3). Here's what the choices mean.

◆ **Smoothing Angle** is the angle above which Infini-D smoothes the edges of polygons. *Always* smoothes all edges, *Never* smoothes no edges, and setting a particular angle tells Infini-D to smooth only polygon edges that meet at an angle greater than the specified degree.

◆ **Scale and Center** resizes the DXF object to fit in the Infini-D window and places it at the center of the World. This is a useful option to have checked, because DXFs vary so much depending on what program originally wrote the file. Often, an unscaled object is imported at a very large size, because Infini-D's unit scale does not always correspond to DXF scale.

◆ **Link Objects** imports objects as linked hierarchies. Linking objects is a good idea. DXF objects sometimes can be imported as individual polygons. Importing unlinked polygons makes handling an object quite difficult.

TIP

If an object is imported as separate polygons, it can be exploded, causing a shattering glass effect. Simply import the DXF with Link Objects unchecked. Select an eventmark for each polygon-object and use the Explode Animation Assistant to blow them apart.

The same effect works with 3DMF files as well, although 3DMF is often broken into larger patches.

You can also explode Infini-D objects this way. Export the object as DXF or 3DMF and re-import it unlinked. Use the Explode Animation Assistant on the resulting polygons or patches.

- **One Object Per Layer** has to do with the way the DXF was exported from the program that created it. *One Object Per Layer* assumes that the file was saved with objects divided into layers.

- **Use Color Info** uses the color information stored in the DXF file. This is about the extent of the surfacing capability of DXF files.

DXF import is a little tricky. Problems may be encountered, depending on the application that wrote the file, or if the file size is unusually large. DXF objects can become complex, and the size increases accordingly. Using the import controls, you can sometimes coerce stubborn files into importing, but if DXF fails entirely, try the more reliable 3DMF.

Importing 3DMF

3DMF's system level support provides multiple ways to import files. QuickDraw 3D treats 3DMF files in the same manner that regular 2D QuickDraw treats PICTs. 3DMF files can be copied and pasted or dragged-and-dropped.

Infini-D supports both methods of file transfer, along with a separate Import command that provides more control over the import parameters.

The options in the 3DMF Import dialog are similar to the DXF options. The only difference is that the 3DMF Import dialog lacks a Use Color Information checkbox. Because 3DMF has more sophisticated surface support, Infini-D always reads the surface information.

Drag-and-Drop

Importing via drag-and-drop is by far the easiest method of importing. Simply select the 3DMF file in the Finder and drag it to an Infini-D window, or drag the object directly from another application into Infini-D. 3DMF files can even be stored in the Scrapbook and retrieved by dragging-and-dropping (a system-wide object library!).

NOTE

System versions prior to 7.5 do not include drag-and-drop support. In order for drag-and-drop to work on these systems, the drag-and-drop extension must be installed.

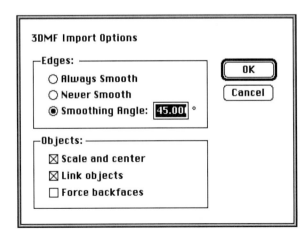

Cut, Copy, and Paste

If drag-and-drop is not an option, cut and paste is nearly as good. The Cut, Copy, and Paste commands are in the Edit menu and perform the same functions as drag-and-drop.

Backface Removal

Whenever Infini-D can, it removes the backs of objects. This saves rendering time by eliminating polygons that are not visible. With DXF and 3DMF, however, it is often difficult for Infini-D to determine which surfaces are on the back of the object and which are facing the viewer. As a result, imported 3D objects sometimes appear inside out. In such cases, Infini-D has accidentally removed the wrong faces, resulting in *frontface removal*. Whenever you are importing 3D objects, it is a good idea to turn on Force Backfaces in the Object Info dialog. Both 3DMF and DXF Import dialogs give you the option to turn on backfaces upon import, and Force Backfaces on is even the default for DXF objects. This tells Infini-D not to remove either side of the object.

Summary

Although some object and surface control is lost when using imported objects, the advantages of multiple modelers are too great to pass up. DXF and 3DMF objects cannot be morphed or edited, and some surfacing techniques, such as decals, don't work, but the number and types of objects that can be built in a variety of different modelers is quite astonishing. Common 3D file formats enable you to take full advantage of any environment.

Animation

Computer animation is currently one of the hottest topics around. Movies like *Jurassic Park, Terminator 2,* and especially *Toy Story* brought computer graphics and animation into the spotlight. While movie effects are generally made with custom software and expensive hardware, Infini-D enables you also to create professional-looking effects and animation. Movies, such as *Memoirs of an Invisible Man, The Mask,* and *Lawnmower Man,* and television shows, such as *Earth 2* and *Babylon 5,* have used Infini-D to create awesome effects. Other movies, such as *Clear and Present Danger* and *Stargate,* have used Infini-D for storyboards and planning. Infini-D's strength in animation stems from its innovative Sequencer and advanced motion controls.

The Sequencer

The concept behind the Sequencer is surprisingly simple yet extremely powerful. Each object in an Infini-D scene has a *timeline* associated with it in the Sequencer. The *World Time Marker* denotes the current point. Animation is created by moving the World Time Marker to different points in time and making corresponding adjustments to objects in the World. Every time you change an object, you create an *event* for that object, which appears on the object's timeline. These *eventmarks* create a sort of itinerary for the objects in your scene, a schedule of where each object is supposed to be at certain times. When animated, the object will move, turn, or morph from one eventmark to the next, changing to match the position, surface, or shape as set at each event. After an eventmark has been made, it can be moved, copied, or deleted. The animation between two eventmarks is represented by a colored connecting stripe.

Events and Sub-Events

As mentioned before, an eventmark represents an object changing its position, orientation, surface, or shape at a particular point in time. It is not, however, immediately clear, by looking at an object's timeline, which attributes have changed. If you change two attributes at the same point in time, such as moving and rotating an object, both of these changes are represented by a single eventmark, and moving that eventmark changes the timing of both. Infini-D has a solution to this problem: double-clicking an object name in the Sequencer reveals the object's sub-parameters—Position, Rotation, Scale,

Centerpoint, Uniform Scale, Surface, and Other Info—each with their own timeline. The timing of specific changes can be made here, independent of the other attributes.

NOTE

Other Info might seem a bit vague at first, but it really is not. While all objects share the attributes of size, scale, and position, some objects have very different properties exclusive to their type. Changes to properties exclusive to a particular type of object are represented in the Other Info timeline. For normal, editable objects, Other Info is where changes to the object's shape are recorded. For Cameras, Other Info is used for the camera's lens type. For lights, this timeline represents color, intensity, and other editable attributes exclusive to lights. Also note that the Surface timeline is never used by either cameras or lights, because neither cameras nor lights can have surfaces applied to them.

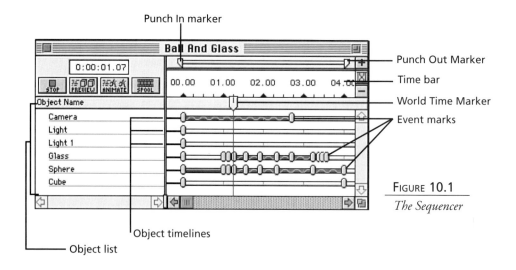

Punch In marker

Punch Out Marker

Time bar

World Time Marker

Event marks

Object timelines

Object list

FIGURE 10.1

The Sequencer

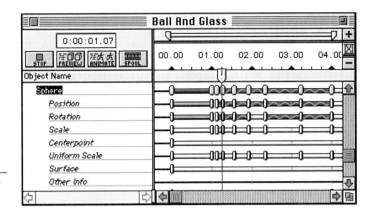

FIGURE 10.2

An object with subparameters revealed.

Manipulating Eventmarks

Both eventmarks and sub-eventmarks can be manipulated in the Sequencer to edit animation. Events can be moved to change the timing, they can be deleted by selecting them and pressing the Delete key, or they be copied by Option-dragging them to another point in time. The same modifications can be made to multiple eventmarks, which can be selected either by Shift-clicking or dragging a marquee around them. With multiple eventmarks selected, an animation sequence can be squashed or stretched by holding the ⌘ key and dragging either the leftmost or rightmost selected eventmark. The relative distance between eventmarks, which represents the relative timing in the animation between those eventmarks, is preserved.

NOTE

Option-dragging an eventmark where an object's shape has changed does not automatically duplicate the Other Info sub-event. To copy an eventmark with an object's shape, you must explicitly copy that object's

Other Info sub-eventmark. This is a convenience in Infini-D, because users reported that, while they frequently copy events, they do object morphing much less often, and only rarely need to copy an object's shape. Because Infini-D can do elaborate morphing between objects, preventing the Other Info sub-eventmark from automatically copying when the other sub-events are duplicated makes it quicker to edit an object without worrying about it suddenly changing shape.

Modifier Keys

After you've started dragging an eventmark or set of eventmarks, two additional modifiers aid in the positioning of events on the timeline. Holding the Shift key snaps the event you're dragging to other events. It is similar to the Snap to Other Points option in the Workshop (which is particularly useful when lining up sub-events with each other). Holding down the Control key while dragging eventmarks works like the Snap to Grid option in the Workshop, automatically snapping the event to ticks on the Sequencer's timeline. Shift and Control also apply to moving the World Time Marker.

Null Events

Sometimes, the most important part of animation is knowing when to remain still. For example, say you want an object to stay where it is for a while, and then move to a new position. If you simply moved the World Time Marker to that time and moved the object to its desired position, the object would start moving immediately when animated. You need a means of instructing the object to remain in the same position until a certain time. *Null events* are the way to do this. Essentially, a null event is the same as any other event, except that it is identical to the one before it. As described earlier, objects move, morph, or otherwise change between eventmarks. Between a normal eventmark and a null eventmark, there is no change.

Create a null event by Option-dragging an eventmark in the Sequencer. If no other events lie between the original eventmark and its copy, the latter is considered a null event.

In the Sequencer, there is no colored bar between a null event and the preceding event. This visually represents that no animation occurs between the two events.

Null events are particularly useful for fine-tuning the animation of sub-events. Suppose, for example, that you are producing an animation of a meteor entering the earth's atmosphere. The meteor is in constant motion, and, as it falls, is heated by atmospheric friction until it begins to burn up. First, create an animation with the meteor at the starting position, full size, with the normal surface, and then create the second event at the meteor's ending position, scaled smaller on the X, Y, and Z axes, and with a hotly glowing surface.

To start the glowing effect, move the meteor's first Surface sub-eventmark forward in time by Option-dragging it. The burning effect is accomplished by Option-dragging the meteor's first Scale sub-eventmark to a point just after the copied Surface sub-event.

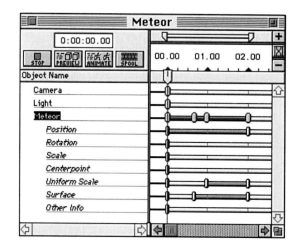

FIGURE 10.3

Using sub-parameters, the comet's position, surface, and scale can be controlled independently.

Snapshots

Snapshots are a quick way to create animation. A snapshot automatically moves the World Time Marker forward along the timeline and creates null events where they are needed. Snapshots can speed up the sequencing of an animation; all you have to do is adjust your objects, take a snapshot (⌘+M), and then adjust them again. Null events are automatically inserted. This ensures that objects do not animate too soon. After you create an animation, you can fine-tune the animation's timing in the Sequencer.

NOTE

While snapshots can be very useful, taking them after you've already created an animation, particularly if the World Time Marker is not at the end of your edited sequence, can cause unexpected problems. When you take a Snapshot, Infini-D assumes that you're either starting your animation from scratch or adding to a sequence already created *with* snapshots. Infini-D might add or remove null events in an unexpected way, which could have strange effects on your final animation.

Birth and Death Events

Birth and death events are the means by which Infini-D causes objects to appear and disappear during animation. Death events cause objects to appear or disappear, keep screen clutter to a minimum by eliminating objects that are not in the camera shot, and decrease rendering time by eliminating objects that are not in the camera shot.

Set a death event by selecting the desired event, double-clicking it, and checking End Animation in the Event Info dialog. After a death event, the object disappears from all rendering modes.

If a death event is followed by a birth event, the Sequencer denotes the object's death with a thin, black bar in the object's timeline instead of the normal gray bar.

It's easy to bring a dead object back to life. Option-drag the death event to duplicate it, edit the new event, and uncheck End Animation. Or, simply change the object later on the timeline. If a dead object, for example, is moved five units to the right one second after the death event, the object dies and reappears five units to the right one second later.

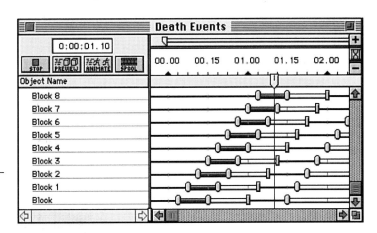

FIGURE 10.4

Dead time is indicated in the Sequencer by a thin, black bar. Death events are rectangular.

An object can change during a death event. A dead object can reappear in a different position, have a different surface, be rotated, scaled, or even have a different shape.

Spline Events

In the Eventmark Info dialog, there are controls that affect the way an object approaches and departs from an event. Events are linear by default, meaning that an object moves straight into the event and departs straight for the next event. If the event, however, is toggled to spline, the object curves smoothly in from the last event, moves smoothly through the event, and curves out toward the next event.

When an event is set to spline, the three controls in the bottom half of the Eventmark Info dialog affect the eventmark. Use the sliders to set tension, bias, and continuity, with the preview on the left as a guide. When using spline

events, turn on motion paths to see how the curves affect the path of your objects. Motion paths are discussed in greater detail later in the chapter.

Linking, Centerpoints, and Constraining

Animation in Infini-D is even easier if objects and scenes are set up with animation in mind. A door, for example, swings on a hinge, or a model made of multiple parts can behave like a single object. Even better, the door can be limited so that it cannot swing through the wall on which it is mounted. If the multi-object model has moving parts, those parts can be limited to sliding back and forth along a track or to spinning a certain way. Specifically, to make animation even easier, Infini-D uses object linking and movable centerpoints, and constrains movement and rotation.

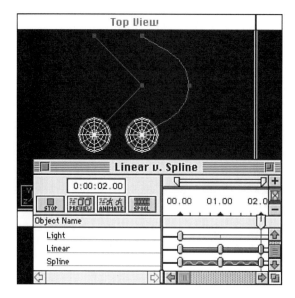

FIGURE **10.5**

The sphere on the left makes sharp corners and sudden movements due to its linear motion. Spline motion makes the sphere on the right move smoothly.

Linking Objects

Object linking is a way to attach one object to another. Infini-D's links form hierarchical parent-child relationships between objects. Child objects are linked to a parent which can be, in turn, linked to its own parent. Children inherit surface information from a parent through the Use Parent's Surface option, and then all position and rotation information becomes relative to the parent.

To link two objects, select the Link tool and click the child object. With the child object selected, click what will be the parent object. Infini-D flashes a line between the two objects indicating that the link was successful. You also can link objects with the Sequencer. Open the Sequencer and select the name of the intended child object. Drag the name onto the name of the parent object. If the link is successful, the child object appears in the Sequencer list as a child of the parent object.

Unlinking is done using the Unlink tool, or in the Sequencer by dragging the child object out of the hierarchy. Release the child name between the parent and the previous object in the list.

There are a number of advantages to linking objects.

◆ **Scene Organization**   Linking objects cleans up the Sequencer list by enabling you to collapse or expand hierarchies as needed. It groups related objects and puts smaller, less important objects inside of hierarchies.

◆ **Hard Locking**   Objects can be *hard locked* to make them behave as though they were a single object. To hard lock an object, link it to a parent and open the Object floater. Select the child. Lock all attributes of the child (holding the ⌘ key while clicking the X, Y, or Z button of any attribute locks all dimensions of that attribute). Now, if a child is selected, it should not move at all. Because the child, however, is relative to the parent, and because the parent is not locked, the child, parent, and any other objects in the hierarchy can move. To make an entire hierarchy behave this way (so that you can click *any* object to move them all), be sure to hard lock all children.

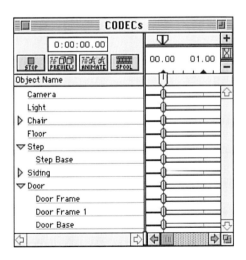

FIGURE 10.6

Object linking builds hierarchies ideal for keeping a scene manageable and tidy.

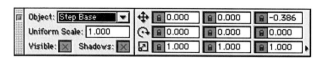

FIGURE **10.7**

Click the axis buttons (X, Y, or Z) to lock a parameter. Hold the ⌘ key to affect all axes at once.

◆ **Easier Scene Manipulation and Animation** Linking makes any scene easier to manipulate and animate. Dragging a parent object moves all of its children, so that moving a multi-part object is as simple as moving the parent. The children are also easier to handle, because all position, rotation, and scale values are relative. Linking makes child objects behave as if they were in a much smaller world based on the parent. For example, instead of guessing what the world unit movement is for an arm when a body walks forward, a relative unit raises the arm while the body walks. Without links, the arm would vary its position relative to the body. Small errors in guessing the approximate position of the arm begin to accumulate and result in poor animation.

◆ **Invisible Parents** In the Object floater, check the box marked Invisible to make an object disappear from the World. A great deal of control over object movement is gained through the use of an invisible parent. An invisible parent is a simple object, such as a sphere, that is invisible and linked to another object or hierarchy of objects. Because the object is invisible, it will not show up in any rendering.

There are many uses for invisible parents. A joint, for example, is much easier to rotate if there are three invisible objects used to control the X rotation, Y rotation, and Z rotation (lock the other two rotations for each parent object). The scale of a surface can be controlled by assigning a surface to the parent, setting the child to Use Parent's Surface, and adjusting the uniform scale of the parent. If you want a character in an animation to look directly at something else, link the head to an invisible camera object. Use Point At in the Model menu to make the character look at another object. As an added bonus, you can open the invisible camera's window and look through the eyes of your own character.

Duplicating as Child

The Duplicate as Child command in Infini-D's Edit menu is one of the least known, yet most useful commands. Using Duplicate as Child, redundant modeling (or models in which an object repeats) is simple. A spiral staircase, for example, contains a repeated object and requires only a few steps to create.

Duplicate as Child maintains the position of the object along with its rotation. Because a child is relative to its parent, repeated duplication produces a chain of objects, each one linked to the previous object.

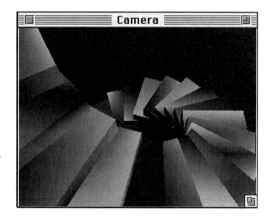

FIGURE 10.8

Spiral staircases and other repeating models can be built easily using Duplicate as Child.

Here's how to create a spiral staircase.

1. **Make a step.** Make any step you like. It can be a squashed primitive cube, an extrude object, or imported from another application.

2. **Make a copy of the step.** Use the regular Duplicate command to make a second step.

3. **Raise the step slightly and rotate it about 20%.** The step needs to be positioned exactly, because the rest of the steps will be based on this one.

4. **Link the second step to the first.** Use the Link tool or, in the Sequencer, drag the second step onto the first.

5. **Select the second step and choose Duplicate as Child.** A third step will form, offset from the second the same way the second is offset from the first. Repeat step five to create additional steps.

Object Centerpoints

The *centerpoint* of an object is the point around which the object revolves and is scaled. In fact, when an object's position is set in the Object floater, it is actually the centerpoint whose location is being set. Despite the name, however, the centerpoint does not have to be in the center of an object.

An object's centerpoint can be moved in two ways. Hold the Control key while dragging an object with the V-plane or H-plane tool to move the object *away* from the centerpoint. The centerpoint stays put while the object is offset.

You also can move the centerpoint in the Workshop. The center of the drawing windows ((0,0) on the rulers) is the center of the object. No matter where the object is placed in the drawing windows, the centerpoint remains at the center of the window. Conversely, if you offset an object's centerpoint in the world, the object is offset from the center of the drawing windows in the Workshop.

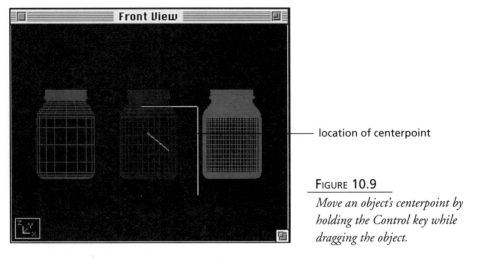

Front View

location of centerpoint

FIGURE **10.9**

Move an object's centerpoint by holding the Control key while dragging the object.

Here are a few of the many uses for moving centerpoints.

♦ **Hinges** To create a flexible joint, such as a hinge or an elbow, create the two halves of the joint and move the centerpoint of the object that rotates to the edge of the joint. In other words, put the centerpoint of the rotating object at the center of rotation. The door will then swing on the hinge, or the arm will bend at the elbow.

♦ **Orbiting objects** Objects that spin around each other, such as planets, can be made by moving centerpoints. To create a moon orbiting the earth, for example, move the centerpoint of the moon to the centerpoint of the earth. Rotate the moon and it will revolve around the earth.

♦ **Growing objects** An object scales from its centerpoint. If the centerpoint is moved, for instance, to the base of the object, the object, when scaled up, will appear to grow up out of the ground. Or, scale the object down to have it shrink down into nothing.

♦ **Center of Interest Cameras** Cameras often need to focus on a specific object while navigating around it. Link the camera to an object and set the centerpoint to (0,0,0). Then, use the Control key to drag the camera from the other object, leaving the centerpoint behind. Now, when you rotate the camera, it still points at the object.

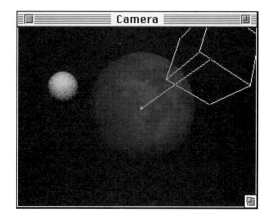

FIGURE 10.10

By placing the centerpoint of the moon at the center of the earth, the moon will rotate around the earth.

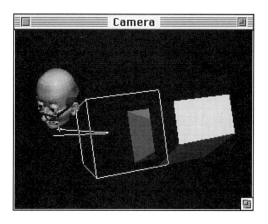

FIGURE 10.11

Focusing a camera or tracking an object is easier when the centerpoint of the camera is the same as that of the object.

◆ **Animating centerpoints** Any changes made to the centerpoint can be animated. Animated centerpoints make it possible to have objects change orbits or cameras change center of interest. Linking cannot be animated, so you'll have to keep the camera unlinked and do positioning by hand.

Constraining

Open the Object floater. In the lower right there's a triangle that, when an object is selected, can be clicked to reveal the constraining controls. These controls limit the movement, rotation, and scale of an object.

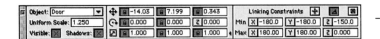

FIGURE **10.12**

The Object floater expands to reveal constraining controls.

To set constraints for an object, set the object to the minimum position, rotation, or scale desired. Expand the Object floater. Select the position, rotation, or scale icon from the top right. Click the X, Y, or Z buttons for the minimum values. Infini-D fills in the current values for each button pressed. Move the object to the maximum position, rotation, or scale and click the appropriate buttons on the maximum row. Values also can be typed in directly.

Constraining can be used for many purposes. An elbow, for example, can be constrained, so that the forearm cannot fold past the upper arm nor extend past a straight position. A computer mouse can be limited to the surface of a mouse pad, and machine parts can be constrained to their possible positions.

Motion Paths and Velocity Graphs

Infini-D 3 added two important controls to Infini-D's already powerful arsenal of animation tools. *Motion paths* are spline-based curves drawn onscreen to represent the motion of an object over time. *Velocity graphs* provide complete control over the acceleration and deceleration of an object attribute. Both are invaluable for producing smooth, realistic motion in animation.

FIGURE **10.13**

These ladders have been constrained, so that they operate like real ladders. The ladder on the left slides up and down, but does not come apart. The step ladder on the right swings open and shut, but only to a specific angle.

Motion Paths

Motion paths display position changes only, not rotation or scale. To turn on motion paths, select any object whose position is, or will be, animated. Choose Enable Motion Path from the Animation menu. A pink path appears, which the object will travel along during the animation. Eventmarks are represented by red dots, and smaller purple dots indicate approximate frames of animation.

The path can be manipulated onscreen. Click a red dot and drag to move the object at that eventmark. Switch views to move the dots in other dimensions. To move the path up or down, for example, use the Front or Right views. Horizontal movements can be made in the Top view.

Spline curves cannot be edited onscreen. To change the curve of an object's motion, select one or more eventmarks and double-click them. The Eventmark Info dialog appears with tension, bias, and continuity sliders. The preview curve above the sliders gives an idea what the curve will look like as you adjust the sliders. Click OK to accept the changes.

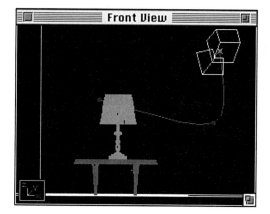

FIGURE 10.14

The path of the camera in this fly-through animation is denoted by the motion path extending from the camera's center.

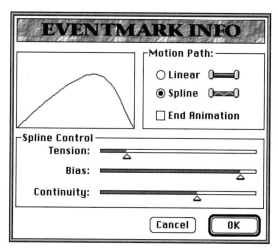

FIGURE 10.15

The Eventmark Info dialog

Motion paths are useful for setting up smooth curves and adjusting motion. Use motion paths to keep track (at a glance) of an object throughout an entire scene, or to edit an object's position without the opening the Sequencer.

Velocity Graphs

Another aspect of smooth motion is acceleration and deceleration. Infini-D does its best to maintain smooth velocity as a scene is animated, but, to truly smooth it out, you'll have to give Infini-D a hand.

1. **Select the object.**

2. **Choose Velocity from the Animation menu.**

3. **Select the attribute whose velocity you wish to adjust.** You can choose position, rotation, centerpoint, scale, or uniform scale.

4. **Adjust the eventmarks as desired.** You can manually adjust each one or use the built-in functions, such as smooth or constant velocity. If you manually adjust events, turn off Auto Velocity to have full control.

Two graphs are provided, so that you can display and compare two attributes at the same time.

Velocity graphs are a mathematical display of an object's rate of movement over a period of time. Because of the mathematics involved, some velocity graph behavior might seem odd. Moving an event up or down to adjust the velocity affects the velocity before and after the curve.

Sometimes large peaks appear in the graph, and other times the graph dips down to the bottom, flattens out, and turns red. Here's why. Velocity is a measure of distance over time. When you move an object from one position to another over a period of one second, you're asking Infini-D to move the object the distance between the two points in one second. If, in the velocity graphs, you move an eventmark to the left, thereby shortening the time between events, Infini-D must perform the same movement in less time. The velocity is increased, and a peak forms in the graph. If the events are spread out, the graph drops as the object slows. If the object slows too much, the graph hits bottom and turns red. Be careful if you see red in the velocity graphs, because there is a good chance that that object is going to move *backward* to accommodate the time you have specified.

To create the smoothest velocity, select a group of events and choose Smooth Velocity. This creates perfectly smooth acceleration and deceleration between events. Constant velocity draws the graph straight across, which indicates no acceleration or deceleration whatsoever. Constant acceleration sets all events in a line, either accelerating or decelerating as necessary, but always at a constant rate. Finally, Average Velocity enables Infini-D to split the velocity, creating average velocities with no acceleration. Split velocity means that the object instantly changes velocity within the space of a single eventmark.

To use any of the presets, drag a selection bar around the desired eventmarks and select a preset from the Magic Wand button. Repeat on other events if necessary.

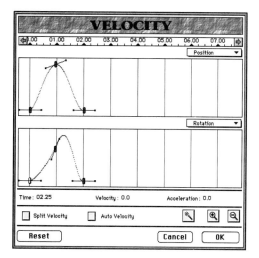

FIGURE 10.16

Infini-D's velocity graphs adjust acceleration and deceleration.

QuickTime VR™

QuickTime Virtual Reality (QuickTime VR or QTVR for short) is a new technology from Apple used to create interactive movies and navigable environments. Infini-D's output can be turned into QTVR movies with Apple's QuickTime VR Authoring Tools suite.

NOTE

Infini-D alone cannot produce navigable, interactive QuickTime VR movies. You need Apple's QuickTime VR Authoring Tools Suite. Infini-D *does*, however, produce output that can be converted quickly and easily, using QTVR Authoring Tools, into interactive QTVR movies.

Using a Panorama as an Environment Map

If you don't have the Apple QuickTime VR Authoring Tools Suite, Infini-D's QTVR functions do not have to go to waste. With little or no post-processing, a panoramic image can be used as an environment map. An environment map gives objects something to reflect, which enhances their shininess and gives the scene more color.

Reflections in an environment map are simulated, however, and the color or shapes reflected in a mirrored object might seem incongruous with the rest of the scene. For a more realistic effect, a panoramic image can be used. This is particularly useful in animation when ray traced reflections may be too time-intensive to use.

FIGURE 10.17

A panoramic render of this scene makes a perfect environment map. The land and sky reflect on the side of the jet without using time-consuming ray tracing to get true reflections.

1. **Place a camera in the center of your scene, orientation (90, 0, 0).** This is the camera used to render the panorama. Make sure the camera is invisible and is not casting shadows.

2. **Set the camera's lens size to 5.** A focal length of 5 is the widest angle lens, approximately 114%. The focal length is set in the View Info dialog (⌘-E).

3. **Render a Panorama.** Render the image twice as wide as tall and with a 360% horizontal pan. Save as a PICT.

4. **Import the rendered panoramic image.** The panoramic image, fresh out of Infini-D, is just a still image. It is no different from any other PICT unless it is processed with Apple's QTVR tools.

5. **Use the panoramic image as an Environment map.** Open the Environment dialog, turn on environment map, and select the panoramic image as the environment.

When rendered, the objects in the scene reflect the environment map. Because the environment map is a panoramic image of the scene itself, objects reflect a 360% image of the rest of the objects around them.

The effect looks best in animated scenes that occur in one place. If the camera moves too far from the place where the panorama was rendered, shiny objects reflect colors and objects that are no longer in that part of the scene.

The effect is not a perfect illusion, but it is pretty good. A perfectly reflective object, if closely examined, will reveal that the reflections aren't real. There are a number of edits you can make to the rendered panoramic image in Photoshop that can improve the effect. Applying a slight blur might make the environment map softer and hide some of the flaws. Also, making sure the top and bottom of the image are a solid color helps eliminate distortion.

The Infini-D environment is one of the easiest to use on any platform. After you master the Sequencer and learn how to plan and build a scene with animation in mind, you'll find the final animation a breeze. Start with some models and surfaces. Use Infini-D's Workshop and powerful surface composition tools. Animate the models, morph the surfaces, adjust the lighting, and build an atmosphere. With a little practice, soon you'll be competing with the pros.

Common Indices of Refraction

MATERIAL	INDEX OF REFRACTION
Air	1.000
Amethyst	1.54
Diamond	2.42
Emerald	1.57
Glass	1.10–1.90
crown	1.52
flint	1.61
Hematite	3.22
Ice	1.31
Oil	
linseed	1.48
olive	1.47
Opal	1.45
Quartz	1.54
Ruby	1.76
Sapphire	1.77
Turquoise	1.61
Water	1.33

Appendix

Smooth QuickTime Playback

Smooth QuickTime movie playback is notoriously difficult. As frame sizes, frame rates, and file sizes increase, playback slows down, becomes jerky, and soundtracks break up as frames are dropped. Aside from buying an expensive hardware accelerator, here are a few things to keep in mind when creating and playing movies.

◆ **Play movies at the same bit-depth with which they were created.** If a movie is saved in 8-bit color (256 colors), it will play most smoothly if the monitor displaying the movie is also set to 8-bit color. A 24-bit movie plays best on a 24-bit monitor. QuickTime movies *can* be played at any bit depth, but the computer slows down as a result of the different color settings.

◆ **Movies with frame dimensions that are multiples of four often compress better than oddly sized frames.** For example, a 320 by 240 pixel movie compresses more efficiently and plays back smoother than a 300 by 200 pixel movie.

◆ **Playing movies from RAM is faster than playing back from a disk.** If you have enough RAM to load the entire movie at once, playback can be much smoother. *Peter's Player* is an excellent movie player that can, space permitting, load a movie completely into RAM. Peter's Player is also optimized in several other ways to provide the smoothest playback possible and is recommended for all your QuickTime playback needs.

Appendix

Reference Materials

◆ *Adobe Photoshop for Macintosh Classroom in a Book*, Copyright ©1994, Adobe Systems Incorporated, Adobe Press.

◆ *Animator's Workbook, The.* Copyright ©1986, Watson-Guptill Publications, a division of Billboard Publications, Inc. Written by Tony White.

◆ *Computer Graphics.* Copyright ©1990, Macmillan Publishing Co., a division of Macmillan, Inc. Written by F.S. Hill, Jr.

◆ *How Did They Do It? Computer Illusion in Film and TV.* Copyright ©1994, Alpha Books, a division of Macmillan Computer Publishing. Written by Christopher W. Baker.

◆ *Macintosh 3-D Workshop.* Copyright ©1993, Hayden Books, a division of Macmillan Computer Publishing. Written by Sean Wagstaff.

Glossary

3D   Three-dimensional. Having, or appearing to have length, width, and depth.

Active view window   The view window that is currently selected. The active view window is marked by six horizontal lines across its title bar.

Algorithm   A step by step method of solving a mathematical problem.

Alpha channel   In a 32-bit image, 8 bits are used for storing the red color information, 8 are used for the green information, and 8 are used for the blue color information. The remaining 8 bits are used by some applications to store masking information for compositing images. A common use is to layer a graphic over a background or an animation over live video. The alpha channel is used to store the anti-aliasing information so that the composite is seamless.

Ambient light   Light that exists everywhere without a particular source. Ambient light does not cast shadows, but fills in the shadowed areas of a scene.

Animate   To give motion to an object or a group of objects over time. In Infini-D, the Sequencer window is used to create and record animation.

Animation   A series of images (called frames) that create an illusion of movement when displayed rapidly in sequence. An animation can be exported as a PICS file, QuickTime movie, or a series of PICT images.

Anti-aliasing   A method of smoothing the jagged edges that appear in computer-generated images when pixels of contrasting colors occur next to one another.

Axis of motion   An imaginary line in 3D space, along which an object moves.

Axis of rotation   An imaginary line in 3D space, around which an object rotates.

Bevel   A bevel removes sharp edges from an extruded object by adding additional material around the surrounding faces. Bevels are particularly useful for flying logos and animation in general, because they reflect additional light from the corners of an object, as well as from the front and sides.

Bitmap   An image composed of specifically colored pixels. A bitmap can be any resolution with any number of colors. The most common bitmap formats are PICT and TIFF.

Bookmark   Just as a real bookmark saves a place in a book, a bookmark in Infini-D saves the position of a viewpoint in the 3D World. After you set a bookmark, you can return to that viewpoint at any time.

Bounding box   A six-sided box drawn onscreen that represents the size of an object. When an object is selected, its bounding box blinks. When this is the selected rendering mode, all objects in the scene are represented only by their bounding boxes.

Bump map   A grayscale image used to give a surface the illusion of ridges or bumps. Infini-D also has a bump generator built in, so that an image is only required when a specific effect is required.

Camera   The object that creates a Camera view window. Like any other object in Infini-D, cameras can be moved, rotated, and animated.

Camera tool   The tool that places cameras in the World.

Camera view   Each camera creates a Camera view window that shows the World from that camera's viewpoint. These views can be opened or closed without affecting the camera.

Center of the World   In World (X, Y, Z) coordinates, the point (0,0,0).

Centerpoint   A point at an object's geometric center. An object's position and rotation are calculated in relation to its centerpoint. An object, however, can be moved from its centerpoint, enabling it to rotate around a point that lies outside itself.

Child   An object that is linked to another object as the child in a parent-child relationship. The motion of the child is influenced by that of the parent.

Color map   An image Infini-D uses to determine the colors of a surface.

Color Picker   The standard Apple dialog box for selecting colors.

Command key (⌘)   The Command key is used with other keys as a shortcut for choosing menu items and to modify the action of tools.

Composed surface   Several surfaces layered together using the Compose Surface dialog box. Surface layers can be built-in procedural surfaces or imported PICT or QuickTime movies.

Constrain   To prevent from moving, rotating, or scaling in one or more directions.

Corrosion map   A pattern that gives a surface a pitted, corroded look.

Cross section   The 2D outline that represents the basic shape of an extrusion in the Workshop. A cross-section can also be thought of as a rib of a lofted object.

Custom object   An object created in Infini-D's Workshop. Custom objects can take any conceivable shape. They are categorized into lathed objects, extruded objects, and SplineForm objects.

Default   For many of Infini-D's features, more than one option is available. When you launch Infini-D, one option is automatically set. The option that is set is called the default, and is in effect until you change the setting.

Diffuse shading   The surface property that determines how much light is scattered in all directions over the surface of an object.

Dimension   The height, width, or depth of an object. To see an object's dimensions, use the Object Information dialog box or the Object floater.

Distant light   A directional light source that does not emanate from a point in space, rather from a direction an infinite distance away. The result is parallel light rays, like sunlight.

Environment Map   An environment map is a surface that is mapped onto a virtual sphere. When an environment map is applied to the World, it is reflected in any reflective objects. Visible detail varies depending on the shading mode selected. Environment mapping is most effective in Phong shading.

Extrusion   The creation of a three-dimensional object by creating a two-dimensional outline giving it height, like a cookie-cutter. It is often used to create 3D text. In Infini-D, extruded objects are created in the Workshop.

Face (Facet)   When a 3D object is created from polygons, a facet is one of the polygons that makes up the surface of an object. Sometimes called *faces*, facets are visible in Wireframe and Fast rendering modes.

Fast shading (Flat)   A fast rendering algorithm that gives each facet of an object a single color. It yields a solid representation of objects without taking a long time to render. It is sometimes referred to as *flat shading*.

Fractal   A mathematically generated pattern that is endlessly complex. Fractal patterns often resemble natural phenomena in the way they repeat elements with slight variations each time. See also **Julia Set** and **Mandelbrot Set**.

Generic primitives   Standard geometric 3D objects: a sphere, cube, cone, cylinder, square, and an infinite plane. Generic primitives often are used as building blocks for making more complex models.

Glow   A surface property that creates the illusion of light emanating from an object.

Gouraud shading (Better)   A rendering algorithm that provides more detail, because it averages color information from adjacent faces to create colors. It is more realistic than fast shading, but less realistic than Phong shading or ray tracing. Gouraud shading is called *Better* in Infini-D.

H-plane tool   The tool in the Toolbox that moves an object left, right, in, and out on a horizontal plane.

Hierarchical model   A model in which objects are linked into object trees. The movement of the child objects depends, in part, on movement of the parent.

Image mapping   A two-dimensional image (in the form of a PICT file) applied to the surface of an object. In Infini-D, you can choose several methods of wrapping a picture around an object. Image mapping is convenient for placing pictures or text onto objects, such as a label on a model or a bottle.

Index of refraction   A ratio that determines the extent to which light bends as it passes through a transparent object.

Infinite plane   A two-dimensional plane, included as one of the six generic primitives, that extends to the World's boundaries.

Julia Set   One of the two fractal patterns available in Infini-D. See also **Fractal**.

Keyframe   A frame in a sequence that specifies all of the attributes of an object. The object can then be changed in any way and a second keyframe defined. The program automatically creates a series of transition frames between the two keyframes in a process called *tweening*. Infini-D uses a modified version of keyframing that is event-driven, which is based upon events in time rather than frames. This enables more flexibility when designing and modifying an animation.

Lathe   A lathe object is created by rotating a two-dimensional shape around a central axis. It is convenient for creating 3D objects like glasses, vases, and bowls.

Layer   One of the surfaces in a composed surface.

Light   An object that emits light. Infini-D offers point lights, spotlights, distant lights, and ambient light.

Light floater   A floating window that enables you to view and modify certain attributes of a light in Infini-D, including light type, color, intensity, and fall-off.

Light tool   The tool in Infini-D's Toolbox that places a light object in the World.

Loft   Lofting (also called *skinning*) stretches a surface over a series of two-dimensional ribs or cross-sections. The surface has the shape of each cross-section and blends smoothly from one to the next. Lofting is the fundamental concept behind Infini-D's Workshop.

Mandelbrot Set   One of the two fractal patterns available in Infini-D. Its name comes from its inventor, the mathematician Benoit Mandelbrot. See also **Fractal** and **Julia Set**.

Map   **1.** To project an image onto the surface of an object. **2.** Images and effects that are applied to a surface to affect its appearance in a certain way (such as marble map, wave map, and so on).

Metallicity   A surface property that determines how much of a surface's color is present in its specular highlight.

Model   Something composed of one or more objects. Models often resemble something in the real world. A guitar model, for example, might contain separate objects for the neck, head, and body of the guitar.

Modeling   Creating and arranging objects, placing lights and cameras, and applying surfaces to objects.

Morphing An abbreviation for metamorphosing, it means to change from one shape to another, usually during an animation.

Motion Path The direction of movement by an object can be represented in the view windows by an onscreen motion path. The path can be directly modified in the windows by dragging the eventmarks on the path.

Movement tools Two tools used to change an object's position in the World. The V-plane tool moves the object on a vertical plane, and the H-plane tool moves the object on a horizontal plane.

Navigation The movement of a view window's point of view. For a camera view, navigation moves the view's camera in the World.

Noise A mathematically defined pattern that uses variable degrees of randomness to generate its color pattern.

Object A single, indivisible entity that can be edited and manipulated in Infini-D. Objects are the building blocks of models.

Object floater A floating window that displays information about an object's position, rotation, and dimensions and enables you to change those values.

Object movie One of the two parts that make up QuickTime VR. Object movies contain an object that can be rotated and examined from almost any angle.

Object tree A group of linked objects. An object tree can contain any number of parent and child objects. A model containing object trees is called a *hierarchical model.*

Option-click To press the Option key while clicking the mouse.

Option key The Option key is used with other keys as a shortcut for choosing menu items and to modify the action of tools.

Orthographic view A view in which an object's distance from the viewer has no effect on the size at which it is drawn. All standard view windows are orthographic views.

Panoramic view A method of rendering through an Infini-D camera in which the camera renders a 360% view around itself. Panoramic rendering outputs files ready to be converted into QuickTime VR movies using Apple's QuickTime VR Authoring Tools Suite.

Parent An object that is linked to another object as the parent in a parent-child relationship. A parent object's coordinates become the center of the World for any of its child objects.

Path The 3D Bézier spline curve in the Workshop that determines the spine of the object. Cross-sections are extruded along the path, and the path passes through the centerpoint of each cross-section.

Perspective view In a perspective view, the farther an object is from the viewer, the smaller it appears. See **Orthographic view**. Camera windows are always displayed in perspective.

Phong shading (Best) A rendering algorithm that creates high-quality surfaces. Phong shading calculates a color for every pixel on an object's surface. The path that the light follows is not calculated in Phong Shading (as it is in ray tracing) so that advanced lighting effects, such as reflection and transparency, cannot be represented. Phong shading is called *Best* mode in Infini-D.

Photorealism A quality in an image that makes it look as though it was created by photography. Originally a technique in painting, photorealism is the result of ray tracing.

PICS file A single Macintosh file consisting of a series of PICT images. In Infini-D, an animation can be saved as a PICS file.

PICT file A standard format used by many Macintosh graphics programs. Any image saved as a PICT file can be imported into Infini-D, and used as a surface, background, or environment map.

Pixel A single dot of light on the computer screen. Short for "picture element," it is the smallest unit of a computer graphic.

Point light A light source that emanates from a single point in all directions, similar to a standard lightbulb. Infini-D has the capability to define how far the light reaches and how quickly it fades.

Procedural shader An algorithm that creates the surface of an object mathematically, rather than from a 2D image. This results in much more realistic objects that look as though they were cut from a solid material. Procedural shaders are commonly used to simulate the veins in a piece of marble or wood. All of the surfaces included with Infini-D are procedural shaders, and users can easily create their own without programming.

QuickDraw 3D™ A technology developed by Apple Computer for handling real time 3D rendering. QuickDraw 3D works at the system level to provide rendering and to facilitate the transmission of 3D data between applications.

QuickTime VR™ A navigable QuickTime movie format developed by Apple Computer. QuickTime VR is made of two parts: object movies and panoramic scenes. Scenes can be linked together to create larger VR spaces, and object movies can be embedded, so that objects in a scene can be picked up and examined.

Rails The two pairs of Bézier spline curves in the Workshop that define the outer shell of an object. Modifying the rails is a way to customize a loft object without the need for many cross-sections.

Ray tracing An intricate rendering algorithm that creates photorealistic images. Ray tracing calculates the path of imaginary rays of light through each pixel on the surface of the objects being viewed. The color for each pixel is determined by how these rays bounce off or are absorbed into an object's surface. Ray tracing can show true reflection, refraction, transparency, and shadows.

Reflectivity A surface property that determines the extent to which an object reflects neighboring objects.

Render To create a three-dimensional representation of an object based on its shape and surface properties.

Rendering mode One of six ways that Infini-D can render objects. The six modes range from Bounding Box, Wireframe, Shade Fast, Shade Better, Shade Best, and ray tracing.

Rotation tools The three tools in the Toolbox that rotate an object in the World.

Scaling tools The two tools in Infini-D that change an object's scale or dimensions. See also **Uniform Scale tool** and **Squash and Stretch tool**.

Scanned images Images, such as photographs or printed illustrations, that have been digitized with a scanner.

Scene A scene includes all of the information about the objects in the World, as well as any new surfaces you have created and any sequence of events you have recorded in the Sequencer. When you save a scene, all of this information is saved in the file.

Sequencer The window in Infini-D that creates, controls, and edits animation. The Sequencer graphically represents any changes to an object as events on a timeline.

Shading The technique of giving the illusion of depth to a surface by varying the color of the polygons that make up that surface.

Shadow The effect of a light source being blocked due to another object in the path between the light and the object. Shadows can be calculated in Phong shading (Best) or ray tracing.

Shift key The Shift key is used to select more than one item at a time (Shift-clicking on Eventmarks, for example) and to constrain movement and tools in various ways.

Shift-click To press the Shift key while clicking the mouse button.

Shininess The shininess of an object can be altered by changing the size and sharpness of a surface's specular highlight.

Skinning See **Loft**.

Specular highlight The distorted reflection of a light source on a shiny object. In general, it has the color of the light source and often appears as a small white spot.

Spotlight A light source that emanates from a point in space in a single direction. Infini-D enables you to define the width of the beam as well as the distance that the light travels.

Squash and Stretch tool The tool that scales an object non-uniformly in one or two of its three dimensions.

Standard view A view whose viewpoint can be moved forward, backward, up, or down (with the Hand tool) but cannot be rotated. There are six standard views: top, front, right, bottom, back, and left.

Surface **1.** The exterior of a three-dimensional object. **2.** All the maps, special effects, and properties designed to simulate the appearance of a specific real-world surface when applied to an object and rendered (for example, glass or brick). Surfaces can be edited, created, and stored in surface libraries. See **Procedural shader** and **Image mapping**.

Surface floater A floating window that provides information about the selected object's surface and special effect map. It also enables you to change or edit the surface.

Surface library Surfaces arranged into a library. Surface libraries can be created, edited, and customized with the Surface Library dialog box. They can also be saved to and opened from files on disk.

Surface properties The characteristics of a material that determine how the material interacts with light.

Sweep Object A sweep object is constructed with a combination of lathing and extruding. As a 2D outline is extruded along the third dimension, it can be assigned an offset distance, a rotation value, and a scaling value. Common sweep objects include springs, corkscrews, and threaded screws. Sweeping is accomplished with the Spiral command in the Workshop.

Three-dimensional Having, or appearing to have, length, width, and depth.

Toolbox A floating window in Infini-D that contains tools for creating and manipulating objects in the Workshop or the World.

Transparency A surface property that determines how much light passes through an object.

Turbulence The extent to which starting and ending colors are shaded across a marble surface.

Uniform Scale tool A tool that causes an object to grow larger or smaller in all directions.

V-plane tool The tool that moves an object left, right, up, and down on a vertical plane.

View What can be seen in the 3D World through one of the view windows. Infini-D has six standard views (top, front, right, bottom, back, and right), and as many camera views as there are cameras in the World. View windows can be opened and closed at will.

View window A window that displays a view of the Infini-D World.

Views floater A floating window that enables you to view and modify the settings of the active view window, including rendering mode, anti-aliasing level, wireframe detail, and bookmarks. The Views floater also contains the rendering progress bar.

Wireframe A representation of a three-dimensional object that shows only the lines of its contours. Wireframe is also a rendering mode in Infini-D that ignores all surface information and is therefore quite fast.

Workshop The Infini-D environment for creating and editing custom objects.

World With each new scene file, Infini-D creates a three-dimensional space called the World. Positions in the World are expressed as coordinates on the World's X, Y, and Z axes. This is where objects are arranged to compose a scene.

World coordinate system A system for representing and recording the position of objects in 3D space. An object's position is given by the X, Y, and Z coordinates of its centerpoint.

World units The units Infini-D uses to determine distances, scaling, and relative size in the World. The measurement system can be changed in the World Preferences dialog box.

X, Y, and Z coordinates The X coordinate of an object is determined by drawing a line, perpendicular to the X axis, from the object's centerpoint to the X axis. The distance from where that line intersects the X axis to the 0 point of the X axis is the object's X coordinate. The Y and Z coordinates are measured in a similar manner.

X, Y, Z axes The three axes of the World's three-dimensional coordinate system. In the Front view, the X axis is an imaginary horizontal line running left to right, the Z axis is a vertical line, and the Y axis is a line that comes out of the screen toward you. In general, any movement parallel to one of these axes is said to be movement along that axis.

Index

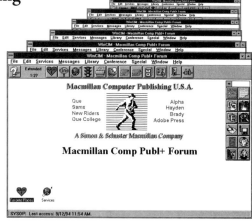

REGISTRATION CARD

Hayden
Books

Infini-D Revealed

Name _____ Title _____

Company_____Type of business _____

Address _____

City/State/ZIP _____

Have you used these types of books before? ☐ yes ☐ no

If yes, which ones? _____

_____

How many computer books do you purchase each year? ☐ 1–5 ☐ 6 or more

How did you learn about this book?_____

☐ recommended by a friend   ☐ received ad in mail
☐ recommended by store personnel   ☐ read book review
☐ saw in catalog   ☐ saw on bookshelf

Where did you purchase this book? _____

Which applications do you currently use? _____

Which computer magazines do you subscribe to? _____

What trade shows do you attend? _____

Please number the top three factors which most influenced your decision for this book purchase.

☐ cover   ☐ price
☐ approach to content ☐ author's reputation
☐ logo   ☐ publisher's reputation
☐ layout/design   ☐ other _____

Would you like to be placed on our preferred mailing list? ☐ yes ☐ no e-mail address _____

☐ **I would like to see my name in print!** You may use my name and quote me in future Hayden products and promotions. My daytime phone number is: _____

Comments _____
_____
_____

Hayden Books Attn: Product Marketing ◆ 201 West 103rd Street ◆ Indianapolis, Indiana 46290 USA

Fax to **317-581-3576**   Visit our Web Page **http://WWW.SuperLibrary.com/hayden/**

Fold Here

- -

‖‖‖‖

BUSINESS REPLY MAIL
FIRST-CLASS MAIL PERMIT NO. 9918 INDIANAPOLIS IN

POSTAGE WILL BE PAID BY THE ADDRESSEE

HAYDEN BOOKS
Attn: Product Marketing
201 W 103RD ST
INDIANAPOLIS IN 46290-9058